GLOBALVIEWPOINTS

Human Trafficking

Other Books of Related Interest:

At Issue Series

Child Labor and Sweatshops

Global Viewpoints Series

Child Soldiers

Human Rights

Women's Rights

Opposing Viewpoints Series

Illegal Immigration

United Nations

GLOBALVIEWPOINTS

Human Trafficking

Margaret Haerens, Book Editor

GREENHAVEN PRESS
A part of Gale, Cengage Learning

GALE
CENGAGE Learning·

Detroit • New York • San Francisco • New Haven, Conn • Waterville, Maine • London

GALE
CENGAGE Learning®

Elizabeth Des Chenes, *Managing Editor*

© 2012 Greenhaven Press, a part of Gale, Cengage Learning

Gale and Greenhaven Press are registered trademarks used herein under license.

For more information, contact:
Greenhaven Press
27500 Drake Rd.
Farmington Hills, MI 48331-3535
Or you can visit our Internet site at gale.cengage.com

Articles in Greenhaven Press anthologies are often edited for length to meet page require-ments. In addition, original titles of these works are changed to clearly present the main thesis and to explicitly indicate the author's opinion. Every effort is made to ensure that Greenhaven Press accurately reflects the original intent of the authors. Every effort has been made to trace the owners of copyrighted material.

Cover image copyright © K. Asif/India Today Group/Getty Images.

LIBRARY OF CONGRESS CATALOGING-IN-PUBLICATION DATA

Human trafficking / Margaret Haerens, book editor.
    p. cm. -- (Global viewpoints)
    Includes bibliographical references and index.
    ISBN 978-0-7377-5658-6 (hbk.) -- ISBN 978-0-7377-5659-3 (pbk.)
    1. Human trafficking--Juvenile literature. I. Haerens, Margaret.
    HQ281.H83 2011
    306.3'62--dc23
                                                                        2011022634

Printed in the United States of America
2 3 4 5 6   15 14 13 12 11
ACC LIBRARY SERVICES AUSTIN, TX

Contents

Chapter 1: Global Trends in Human Trafficking

Contents

Chapter 1: Global Trends in Human Trafficking

Chapter 2: Factors Contributing to Human Trafficking

Chapter 3: Strategies to Reduce Human Trafficking

A recent report by the Drugs and Crime Prevention Committee in Victoria elucidates the failure of the political and law enforcement community to deal effectively with the problem of human trafficking. The inquiry was limited; a more constructive report would have included human trafficking in all its forms.

Chapter 4: Aiding the Victims of Human Trafficking

A nongovernmental organization working in Ghana, the Centre for the Initiative Against Human Trafficking (CIAHT), is working to help the victims of human trafficking reintegrate into society. The organization provides medical and psychological assistance, job-skills training, and business loans to victims.

Foreword

*"The problems of all of humanity can
only be solved by all of humanity."*
—*Swiss author Friedrich Dürrenmatt*

Global interdependence has become an undeniable reality. Mass media and technology have increased worldwide access to information and created a society of global citizens. Understanding and navigating this global community is a challenge, requiring a high degree of information literacy and a new level of learning sophistication.

Building on the success of its flagship series, Opposing Viewpoints, Greenhaven Press has created the Global Viewpoints series to examine a broad range of current, often controversial topics of worldwide importance from a variety of international perspectives. Providing students and other readers with the information they need to explore global connections and think critically about worldwide implications, each Global Viewpoints volume offers a panoramic view of a topic of widespread significance.

Drugs, famine, immigration—a broad, international treatment is essential to do justice to social, environmental, health, and political issues such as these. Junior high, high school, and early college students, as well as general readers, can all use Global Viewpoints anthologies to discern the complexities relating to each issue. Readers will be able to examine unique national perspectives while, at the same time, appreciating the interconnectedness that global priorities bring to all nations and cultures.

Material in each volume is selected from a diverse range of sources, including journals, magazines, newspapers, nonfiction books, speeches, government documents, pamphlets, organization newsletters, and position papers. Global Viewpoints is truly global, with material drawn primarily from international sources available in English and secondarily from US sources with extensive international coverage.

Features of each volume in the Global Viewpoints series include:

- An **annotated table of contents** that provides a brief summary of each essay in the volume, including the name of the country or area covered in the essay.

- An **introduction** specific to the volume topic.

- A **world map** to help readers locate the countries or areas covered in the essays.

- For each viewpoint, an **introduction** that contains notes about the author and source of the viewpoint explains why material from the specific country is being presented, summarizes the main points of the viewpoint, and offers three **guided reading questions** to aid in understanding and comprehension.

- **For further discussion** questions that promote critical thinking by asking the reader to compare and contrast aspects of the viewpoints or draw conclusions about perspectives and arguments.

- A worldwide list of **organizations to contact** for readers seeking additional information.

- A **periodical bibliography** for each chapter and a **bibliography of books** on the volume topic to aid in further research.

- A comprehensive **subject index** to offer access to people, places, events, and subjects cited in the text, with the countries covered in the viewpoints highlighted.

Global Viewpoints is designed for a broad spectrum of readers who want to learn more about current events, history, political science, government, international relations, economics, environmental science, world cultures, and sociology—students doing research for class assignments or debates, teachers and faculty seeking to supplement course materials, and others wanting to understand current issues better. By presenting how people in various countries perceive the root causes, current consequences, and proposed solutions to worldwide challenges, Global Viewpoints volumes offer readers opportunities to enhance their global awareness and their knowledge of cultures worldwide.

Introduction

> *"This is modern slavery. A crime that spans the globe, providing ruthless employers with an endless supply of people to abuse for financial gain."*
>
> *—US Secretary of State Hillary Clinton*

In September 2010 the US government filed charges against six recruiters from a Los Angeles–based recruiting company for human trafficking, thereby launching the biggest human trafficking case to date in the United States. The company, Global Horizons, is accused of luring four hundred laborers from Thailand to the United States and then forcing them to work, often without their promised wages and under poor conditions. Once the workers came to America in May 2004, employees of the company confiscated their passports, threatened them with deportation, and even beat them. They were then sent to farms in Hawaii, Washington, California, Colorado, Massachusetts, New York, and several other states and were forced to work long hours at grueling manual labor.

The Global Horizons case is the most prominent and publicized in a string of human trafficking cases in the United States in recent years. The Thai workers who fell victim to Global Horizons were forced into labor picking fruit and vegetables on farms all over the country. Unfortunately, that case is only the tip of the iceberg when it comes to the problem of human trafficking in the United States. The US Department of State estimates that approximately 17,500 people are trafficked to and within America every year; others estimate there are as many as 60,000 victims every year. As Federal Bureau of Investigation (FBI) special agent Tom Simon commented after the Global Horizon arrests, "There are more people living in forced labor today than when President Lincoln signed the Emancipation Proclamation," which led to the freeing of slaves in the late nineteenth century.

Forced labor is the most common type of human trafficking in the United States. Other forms of human trafficking include sex trafficking, which involves forced prostitution, stripping, and pornography; involuntary domestic servitude, or the exploitation of domestic help; and child sex trafficking. Additional forms of human trafficking found in other parts of the world include child soldiery, which involves kidnapping children and forcing them to fight in armed conflicts; organ trafficking, which is the forced donation of organs for financial gain; and bonded labor, in which an individual or entire family goes into servitude to pay off a high-interest loan.

Human trafficking is a concern not only in the United States; it is a massive international problem. In fact, it is one of the fastest growing types of transnational crime worldwide. According to the US State Department's 2009 "Trafficking in Persons Report," at least 12.3 million adults and children fall victim to human traffickers every year. There have been cases on every continent and in countries as isolated and unpopulated as Iceland. It is a lucrative criminal industry, bringing in $5–9 billion of annual revenue, with profits expected to rise sharply in coming years.

One reason that human trafficking is booming is globalization. As countries become integrated into a global network connected by technology, trade, and culture, economic disparities deepen. Corporations and companies now competing in a global marketplace need cheap labor—and it does not matter where it comes from. This means a rise in the number of dishonest employment recruiters and abusive and exploitative employers actively looking in impoverished areas to fill the increasing need for labor. Men and women are more willing to migrate in order to find work. Sex tourism has also been on the rise, leading to rings of sex traffickers recruiting young women and boys into forced prostitution and other sex work. As Louise Shelley maintains in her book *Human Trafficking: A Global Perspective*, the demand for human trafficking has "increased as producers depend more on trafficked and exploited labor to stay competitive in a global economy in which consumers seek cheap goods and services, including easily available and accessible sexual services."

Another factor that has led to a sharp increase in human trafficking is the global economic downturn. In the late 2000s, the United States fell into a deep economic recession. The American housing market collapsed, large financial institutions failed, businesses closed, state and local government revenues fell, the stock market plummeted, and consumer spending plunged. With the global interconnectivity of today's modern economy, the impact of the US economic problems reverberated in every corner of the globe. Despite the coordinated efforts of political leaders, national ministers of finance, and central bank directors, by the end of October 2008 countries all over the world were facing their own economic crises.

The global economic downturn led to more people at risk. In its 2009 global employment report, the International Labour Organization estimated that the recession could result in more than 200 million workers, mostly in developing economies, being thrust into extreme poverty—a desperate situation that makes more people vulnerable to both labor and sex trafficking. Plus, with the increasing demand for cheaper goods and services, human trafficking cemented its position as one of the most common transnational crimes in the modern era. As the 2009 "Trafficking in Persons Report," confirmed, "A striking global demand for labor and a growing supply of workers willing to take ever greater risks for economic opportunities seem a recipe for increased forced labor cases of migrant workers and women in prostitution."

With the two related factors of globalization and the global recession working to increase the practice of human trafficking, countries struggle to confront the problem. In the United States, the FBI opened 132 trafficking investigations, made 139 arrests, and obtained 94 convictions in 2008. American officials have made human trafficking a top priority in law enforcement. Other countries have stepped up their efforts to identify, catch, and prosecute human traffickers. For example, Great Britain has vowed to procure more convictions for human trafficking. Egypt has set up the National Coordinating Committee to Combat and Prevent Trafficking in Persons, which has improved enforcement of the country's anti-trafficking laws. Several countries, including Kenya and Sweden, have passed recent laws to curb sex and labor trafficking. On an international level, the United Nations (UN) has intensified its efforts on trafficking issues. The UN Global Plan of Action to Combat Trafficking in Persons was created to coordinate and strengthen efforts of member states to eliminate the global scourge of human trafficking.

Even California, where the Global Horizons case was based, has taken decisive action to address the problem. In October 2010 the state passed a law, known as the California Transparency in Supply Chains Act, which requires manufacturers and retailers in the state to disclose their efforts to ensure that every link in their supply chains are free of slavery and forced labor. These initiatives must be posted in full on the companies' websites. Officials and activists hope that this forces companies to reexamine their practices from top to bottom and remain vigilant against human trafficking. "Trafficking is the worst of humanity and takes vigilance to eliminate," observed California governor Arnold Schwarzenegger at the law's signing. "Slavery still exists."

The authors of the viewpoints presented in *Global Viewpoints: Human Trafficking* discuss the worldwide problem of human trafficking, including the effect that the global economic downturn has had on the transnational crime. The viewpoints in this book provide an overview of several political, economic, and cultural factors that contribute to human trafficking and examine strategies that international organizations, national and local governments, and nongovernmental organizations are utilizing to address trafficking in their regions of the world.

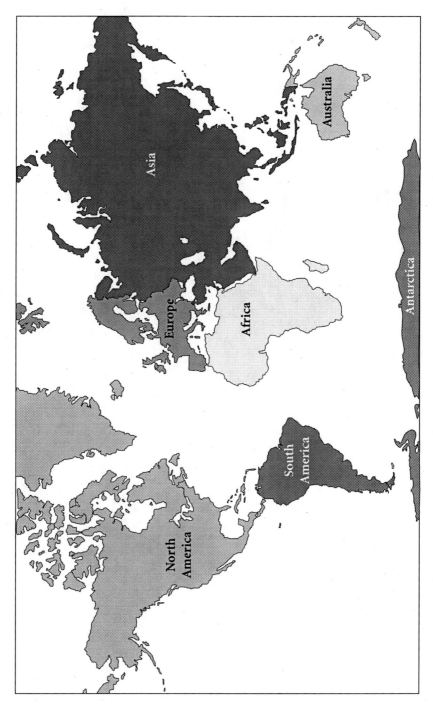

CHAPTER 1

Global Trends in Human Trafficking

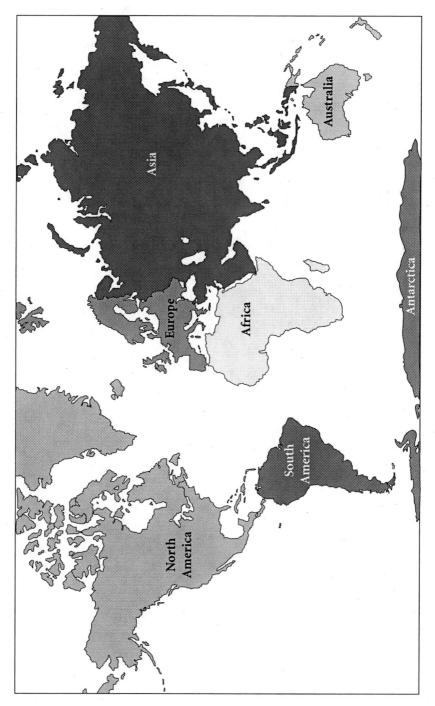

**GLOBAL**VIEWPOINTS

CHAPTER 1

Global Trends in Human Trafficking

Europe Is Plagued by Human Trafficking

Amanda Price

Amanda Price is a reporter at Deutsche Welle, Germany's international broadcaster. In the following viewpoint, she takes the opportunity of the European Union's annual Anti-Trafficking Day to reflect on the problem of human trafficking, which she calls a pan-European crime. Price notes that European officials are not happy with the number or quality of trafficking prosecutions, and she reports that law enforcement has shifted its focus to procuring victims' testimonies, which are difficult to get for a variety of reasons.

As you read, consider the following questions:

1. What countries are among the favored destinations for trafficking?

2. According to Germany's Federal Criminal Police Office, how many criminal investigations were there into human trafficking that involved sexual exploitation in 2009?

3. How many estimated victims of human trafficking are there worldwide every year?

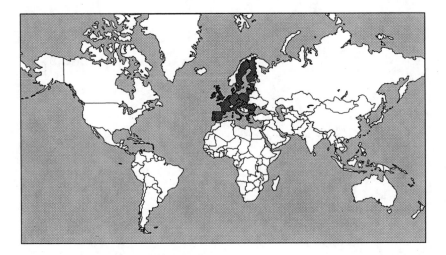

Several hundred thousand people are still being trafficked into or within the European Union [EU] annually—a form of modern-day slavery.

And more than ever, human trafficking today is a pan-European problem.

With the motto "time for action," the first EU Anti-Trafficking Day was established on October 18, 2007, upon recommendation from the European Parliament and an EU Commission proposal.

Now as the bloc marks the fourth annual day against human trafficking in 2010, European law enforcement is putting the focus on prosecution of the perpetrators.

"We're not seeing the number of cases coming to court that we would like," Steve Harvey, Europol's regional support officer for southeast Europe and the Balkans, told Deutsche Welle.

The Challenges in Bringing Traffickers to Justice

Bringing human traffickers to justice can be a tricky proposition. Smuggling human beings across national borders for sexual and labour exploitation is a complex crime, and efforts to collect evidence can be particularly challenging.

Victims' testimonies are invaluable to help stop the crime, yet these persons are already in a vulnerable position. Most are afraid to talk about their experiences because they fear both deportation from the country they have been trafficked to as well as repercussions from traffickers.

Law enforcement is complicated because traffickers are operating in international networks.

Smuggling human beings across national borders for sexual and labour exploitation is a complex crime, and efforts to collect evidence can be particularly challenging.

"Traffickers are professional criminals," Harvey said, adding that most perpetrators are also involved in other areas of organized crime and make every effort to obstruct the investigation.

Harvey said Europol and other law enforcement agencies must target crime bosses, keeping in mind that arresting street criminals and lower-level traffickers might not impact larger crime networks.

"Given that the trafficking is inherently cross-border, we need to ensure that the local, regional and national investigations are developed to their best potential," he said.

The "cross-border" nature of the problem means that while certain cities and countries, like Germany or Britain, are still favored destinations for smugglers, trafficking is no longer a matter of geographic "hot spots."

"A few years ago, you could probably pick up a map of Europe and draw some arrows and lines, and chart the routes that people take across Europe," Harvey said.

"I don't think that's relevant anymore."

Country of Origin of Persons Trafficked to Europe

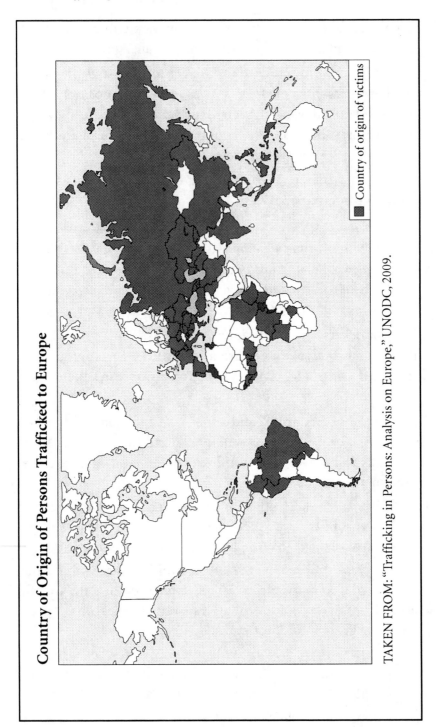

Country of origin of victims

TAKEN FROM: "Trafficking in Persons: Analysis on Europe," UNODC, 2009.

Under the Radar

Western European countries are among the favoured destinations for trafficking: In a recent case in Germany, police identified at least 50 victims of human trafficking—many of them from Nigeria—after searching some 600 brothels nationwide.

Meanwhile, Frankfurt police officer Markus Steiner told Deutsche Welle that even when police raids in the city turn up empty-handed, it doesn't always spell good news.

"That doesn't mean that there will be fewer victims from human trafficking," he said. "This only means that the victims will be sent to other cities like Hanover, Hamburg, Stuttgart, Munich and elsewhere in Germany."

In August [2010], police in Bonn arrested a band of human traffickers from Bulgaria that was bringing young women to Germany and forcing them to work as prostitutes.

"The women were staying in rented rooms, mostly in older hotels. They had to share a room with several women, so the hygienic conditions were poor," head investigator Rainer Bell told Deutsche Welle.

"It looks as if the women work the streets 12 to 14 hours on average—in Cologne or Bonn—and only came home to sleep, day after day."

Statistics released by Germany's Federal Criminal Police Office for 2009 indicated there were 534 criminal investigations into human trafficking involving sexual exploitation—an increase of 11 percent. The number of victims was up 5 percent over the previous year, with 710 reported.

Trafficking Worldwide

Yet the hidden nature of human trafficking means there are no firm numbers on just how many people become victims annually—a problem that is also reflected on an international level.

Estimates put the figure at between 700,000 and four million worldwide each year, according to Jean-Philippe Chauzy, a spokesman for the International Organization for Migration.

"Human trafficking, either for sexual or labor exploitation, is truly a global phenomenon," he told Deutsche Welle. "There are no regions of the world that are not affected by trafficking."

The hidden nature of human trafficking means there are no firm numbers on just how many people become victims annually—a problem that is also reflected on an international level.

Chauzy said that migrants—including women and children—who leave home in search of better lives often have few chances to emigrate legally, prompting them to take risks that could make them vulnerable to traffickers.

"In many cases, unfortunately, they find themselves in situations of exploitation," he said.

It's something that Alina Buteci, a consultant at European anti-trafficking network "La Strada" sees all too often. In the Moldovan capital Chisinau, she receives phone calls from people who are looking for work abroad—and from people looking for family members who are nowhere to be found.

"There are also the relatives of people who are missing, who became victims of smugglers," she said. "They need our help to find their relatives and to bring them back."

Out of some 30,000 calls made to the organization's hotline through the summer of 2009, La Strada said more than 1,000 involved missing persons—and presumed cases of human trafficking.

The Philippines Is a Center for Human Trafficking

Girlie Linao

Girlie Linao is a reporter for the Kuwait Times. *In the following viewpoint, Linao contends that the Philippines has a continuing problem with human trafficking because of the global popularity of Filipino men, women, and children as domestic workers, a practice encouraged by the Philippine government. Linao argues that many women and children recruited as domestic workers are particularly vulnerable and often end up as forced labor or prostitutes without any resources to help them.*

As you read, consider the following questions:

1. When did the Philippines' status on human trafficking improve?
2. On which individuals do recruiters often prey, according to Cecilia Flores-Oebanda?
3. Why do some of the victims get angry at the very organizations trying to help them?

The modus operandi is almost always the same—sweet-talking recruiters entice parents to allow their young daughters to leave the provinces and work in Manila as do-

Girlie Linao, "Stark Reality of Human Trafficking in Philippines," *Kuwait Times*, March 3, 2007. Reproduced with permission.

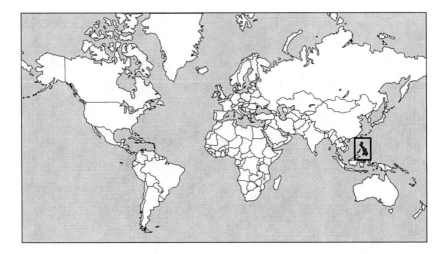

mestic helpers with promises of huge salaries. But once the girls arrive in Manila, the story turns sour with many of them ending up in forced labour or prostitution. Worse, they are "trained" for "export" to other countries as far as the Middle East to work as prostitutes. "Trafficking in the Philippines has two faces—one is for local consumption and the other for abroad," said Cecilia Flores-Oebanda, president of Visayan Forum Foundation, a nongovernmental organisation working for the welfare of migrants.

"Women are first recruited to Manila, where they are trained for deployment abroad," she said. "They are taught how to undress, they are bleached, beautified, then initiated into the sex trade with foreigners as their first customers." "That's what they call on-the-job training while their papers are fixed for travel abroad," she [said] in an interview. As the government and such organisations as Visayan Forum step up the fight against human trafficking, the lure of a better life, a culture that accepts child labour as long as parents consent to it, abject poverty and the government's labour-export policy still fuel the modern-day slavery and lead to estimated tens of thousands of Filipinos, mostly women and children, being trafficked every year.

The Philippines Makes Progress in the Fight Against Trafficking

Due to its continued notoriety as a source, transit and destination country for trafficked persons, the Philippines has remained on the US State Department's tier 2 list of countries that do not fully comply with international standards against human trafficking but are making significant progress to fight the problem. The Philippines used to be in the tier 2 watch list but saw its status improve in 2006 after seven of 186 legal cases filed from 2003 to 2006 resulted in convictions. Oebanda said the Philippine government's continued deployment of Filipino workers, mostly as domestic helpers, around the world, whose wages are a much-needed source of revenue for the country, was exposing Filipino women and children to the dangers of trafficking.

The Philippines has remained on the US State Department's tier 2 list of countries that do not fully comply with international standards against human trafficking but are making significant progress to fight the problem.

She noted that even Filipinos with overseas work permits could end up being trafficked. "Some of them secure work permits, but is their job really the work that they asked the permit for?" she asked. "We are worried and alarmed that our major source of income is people that we send out as migrants. We lack protective mechanisms and this adds to the vulnerability of people." Oebanda said recruiters often prey on young women between 12 and 22 years old. The victims are usually school dropouts, looking for jobs or a way out of the provinces. "Some women just want to get out of the provinces," she said. "They want to come to Manila or any urban centre. They flock to urban centres, where there is a perceived notion of better opportunities waiting for them."

Human Trafficking in the Philippines

Currently, the Philippines is one of the largest migrant countries in the world. A percentage of this large migrant population comprises illegal migrants. Some of these are victims of human trafficking. In spite of the existence of legal channels for overseas employment in the Philippines, intermediaries who offer their services for the expeditious but illegal alternatives continue to exist, and this contributes to the problem of trafficking. Victims are subject to contract violations regarding pay and working conditions, are deceived about the nature of work they will have to undertake after arrival in the destination country, are forced into sexual contact with customers, and subjected to various forms of coercion, manipulation, physical and sexual assaults.

United Nations Office on Drugs and Crime,
"Trafficking in Human Beings from the Philippines: A Survey
of Government Experts and Law Enforcement Case Files," 2008.

The Case of Gladys

Gladys, 19, left her home province of Surigao del Norte in the southern Philippines for the central city of Cebu in the hopes of finding a job to help her poor family. The youngest girl in a brood of five said she was recruited by a relative to work as a domestic helper but ended up as a waitress in a nightclub frequented by foreign tourists in a red-light district in Cebu City. "I wanted to experience life in a city and how it is like to have a job," she [said]. "I also thought that if I can work, it would be a great help to my parents."

Dressed in skimpy attires every night, she often receives indecent proposals from customers who grab and touch her even without her consent while serving drinks or food at their tables. For three months, the advances escalated, and she said she feared she would end up like other girls in the bar who not only work as waitresses but also dance half-naked and perform sexual services. Unable to stand the exploitation, she approached Visayan Forum and asked for help. She is now undergoing computer training to help her achieve her goal of becoming a teacher. Other girls are not as lucky as Gladys. In some cases, Visayan Forum has rescued young women locked up in rooms where they are forced to have sex with as many as 20 men every night.

Even women who end up working as domestic helpers also sometimes face sexual abuse from their male bosses.

"The operator of the prostitution house counts the men the girls had serviced by the number of condoms on the floor," Oebanda said. Even women who end up working as domestic helpers also sometimes face sexual abuse from their male bosses. Elena was only 15 when her parents traded her for 500 pesos ($10) to a recruitment agency in the southern province of Misamis Oriental. In one of her many jobs as a domestic helper, Elena was raped repeatedly by her male employer when his wife went on vacation to the United States. The abuse continued for quite some time until she was let go by the couple and returned to the recruitment agency. "When I asked for help from my recruiter, I was merely told that since I was no longer a virgin, I might as well become a sex worker," she told Visayan Forum. "I was so furious, I escaped, not knowing where I'd end up."

While most of those rescued are grateful for the help, Oebanda said some of the women and children have been so hardened by their ordeal that they get angry at social workers like her. "They see us as getting in their way, that we're taking away their jobs and opportunities," she said. "Some of them even vandalize our shelters. But eventually they appreciate it."

Iceland Addresses Its Human Trafficking Situation

Lowana Veal

Lowana Veal is a reporter for Inter Press Service (IPS) news agency. In the following viewpoint, she maintains that the overwhelming majority of Icelanders have been relatively unaware of the problem of human trafficking—particularly within their own borders—until a recent case of sex trafficking ignited a firestorm of controversy and opened Icelanders' eyes to the crime. Veal suggests that human trafficking in Iceland has gone unnoticed for so long because the government has failed to take the crime seriously. To effectively address it, government officials must funnel money and training into programs that identify and help victims.

As you read, consider the following questions:

1. According to Frida Ros Valdimarsdottir, how many cases of human trafficking did she identify in Iceland from 2007–2010?

2. Why does Valdimarsdottir claim that so few cases get to the police for prosecution?

3. What legislation did Iceland's parliament pass in March 2010?

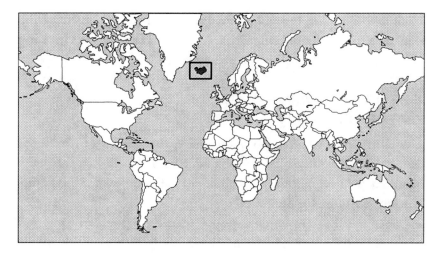

It took the conviction of five Lithuanian men in March [2010], on charges of bringing a 19-year-old girl into Iceland for sex work, before this country truly woke up to the reality of trafficking.

In what became Iceland's first convictions for trafficking, the Lithuanian men were sentenced to five years each in jail on Mar. 8.

Yet, the Lithuanian case may have gone unnoticed except that the victim showed signs of distress while on the plane that brought her to this country last October.

It took the conviction of five Lithuanian men in March [2010], on charges of bringing a 19-year-old girl into Iceland for sex work, before this country truly woke up to the reality of trafficking.

Suspicion aroused, police soon discovered that she was travelling on false documentation and that she had already been forced into prostitution in Lithuania.

"The girl had never flown before. She had been provided with a ticket and told she was going to Iceland, but she didn't know where Iceland was and thought she could hitch a ride back home with a truck driver," Hildur Jonsdottir, chair of the National Coordination Unit Against Human Trafficking (NCUAHT), told IPS [Inter Press Service].

Raising Awareness About Human Trafficking

Gudrun Jonsdottir from Stigamot, a women's centre for survivors of sexual abuse and violence, told IPS: "It has taken 10 years to get the public in Iceland to become aware that trafficking exists in Iceland too."

"We get 30–40 people a year because of pornography and prostitution-linked services," she added. However, very few foreign women come to Stigamot. "Their bosses do not want them to come to us," continued Jonsdottir.

Jonsdottir says there are varying definitions of human trafficking. Stigamot adheres to the definition provided by the Palermo Convention [referring to the United Nations Protocol to Prevent, Suppress and Punish Trafficking in Persons, Especially Women and Children], which says that the distinction between pornography, prostitution and trafficking is unclear.

Under the Palermo definition, trafficking can occur within a country as well as between countries, and can be prostitution or other forms of sexual exploitation, which could extend to strip clubs.

Frida Ros Valdimarsdottir, a specialist working in the field of human trafficking and sex work prevention who has identified 59–128 cases of trafficking over the last three years [2007–2010], says that cases seldom reach the police.

"People do not always define themselves as victims of trafficking—in reality this happens only occasionally—so it is more of an interpretation on my part and less on that of my interviewees," she says.

Valdimarsdottir built her work on interviews with government employees, community associations and similar organisations and, like Stigamot, stuck to the Palermo definition.

"It is a known fact that when governments begin to take trafficking seriously and work on measures for victims, more people seek advice from them than from the police. So I am not surprised that more people feel it is more beneficial to look for support and help from government institutions than from the police," she added.

The Human Trafficking Problem Is Not Insignificant

Valdimarsdottir points out that while the number of trafficking cases in Iceland is far lower than in other countries, it does not necessarily mean that the problem is small. "It is much more likely that the Icelandic government had failed to act on this issue until the case of the Lithuanian girl came up at the end of last year. Government officials have actually admitted this," she said.

Another case of trafficking that compelled the government to sit up and take notice centres on a young woman from Equatorial Guinea, now an Icelandic citizen, who was initially charged with trafficking, importing illegal drugs into Iceland and operating a brothel, but was acquitted of the trafficking charge.

A few days later she was charged again for trafficking and the case is currently under judicial process. One consequence of the prosecutions is that Althingi, Iceland's parliament, now governed by Social Democrats and Left-Greens, finally passed legislation in March banning striptease shows and clubs. Earlier a Left-Green politician had tried to bring about a ban but failed. The no-stripping legislation followed another last year aimed at prosecuting buyers of sex services, on the Swedish pattern. Some of the clients of the Equatorial Guinean woman have been identified and will be brought to trial.

Plans are on to help the victims of trafficking under a series of 25 new measures being implemented by NCUAHT. About 10–12 of these have already been implemented while others, such as those on providing information and setting up a registration system, are in the pipeline.

"Implementation has occurred incredibly quickly," informs Jonsdottir. "Target professional groups such as the police and lawyers will be provided with information, but it is also important for people like flight attendants to be fully informed," she said.

Zimbabwe Is a Major Route for Human Trafficking

Paidamoyo Muzulu

Paidamoyo Muzulu is a reporter for the Zimbabwe Independent. *In the following viewpoint, Muzulu cites Zimbabwe as a major center for human trafficking in southern Africa, with many victims passing through the country on their way to South Africa, which is the main destination in the region for trafficking victims. Muzulu argues that anti-trafficking efforts have been stymied by political chaos, economic strife, and a paucity of laws against the practice, leaving the country vulnerable to the scheming of criminal gangs and corrupt officials.*

As you read, consider the following questions:

1. How much does human trafficking rake into sub-Saharan Africa every year, according to the viewpoint?
2. Why does the author think that trafficking is prevalent in the SADC region?
3. According to International Organization for Migration statistics, how many victims of trafficking were identified and assisted between January 2004 and April 2010 in Zimbabwe?

Zimbabwe has become one of the major routes in Sadc [Southern African Development Community] for human trafficking, with most victims passing through the country on

Paidamoyo Muzulu, "Zim a Major Route for Human Trafficking," *Zimbabwe Independent*, October 21, 2010. Reproduced by Permission.

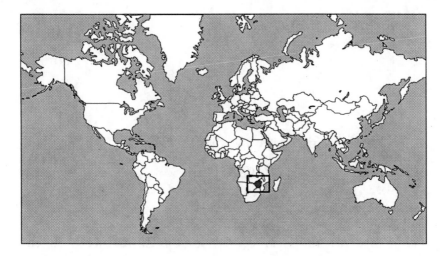

their way to South Africa. It is a trade that is raking in an estimated US$1.6 billion annually in sub-Saharan Africa due to lack of laws that criminalise it.

Defining Human Trafficking

The United Nations [UN] protocol on trafficking defines human trafficking as the recruitment, transportation, transfer, harbouring or receipt of persons by means of a threat or use of force or other forms of coercion, abduction, fraud, deception, abuse of power, a position of vulnerability or of the giving or receiving of payments or benefits to achieve the consent of a person having control over another person, for the purpose of exploitation.

Trafficking of persons in the Sadc region is fuelled by the prevalent unemployed youthful population, great economic disparities, and porous borders, and the region's diverse range of human trafficking activity from the global operations of transnational criminal organisations to small-scale local syndicates that recruit acquaintances, friends and family members.

South Africa is commonly regarded as the main country of destination for trafficked persons in the region. In many cases, women and children are lured to South Africa with promises of jobs, education, or marriage only to be sold and sexually exploited in the country's major urban centres, or in small towns and more rural environments. There is also some indication that men are being trafficked into that country for purposes of forced labour, particularly in the agricultural sector.

Women and children are lured to South Africa with promises of jobs, education, or marriage only to be sold and sexually exploited in the country's major urban centres, or in small towns and more rural environments.

Legislation Is Needed to Address the Problem

However, human trafficking remains a largely clandestine activity perpetrated by criminal groups, and there are presently no laws in the region which focus specifically on the crime of trafficking. As a result, few reliable statistics on human trafficking in southern Africa are available.

Yukiko Kumashiro, International Organization for Migration (IOM) Zimbabwe programme support officer, said only a few cases have been handled at the Beitbridge border post due to legislative loopholes in the country's statutes.

"In terms of trafficking in person cases, there was only one case identified among the Beitbridge returnees in 2008. From the IOM assessment conducted in 2009–2010 in Musina/Beitbridge, it seems that migrants are more subject to smuggling of persons in that area, as well as other kinds of exploitation like sexual and gender-based violence and crimes," said Kumashiro.

"It is however noted that the identified trafficking cases by IOM are only a drop in the ocean, particularly in light of lack of concrete legal framework on trafficking and case reporting mechanisms."

Human Trafficking in Zimbabwe

Zimbabwe is a source, transit, and destination country for men, women, and children trafficked for the purposes of forced labor and sexual exploitation. Large-scale migration of Zimbabweans to surrounding countries—as they flee a progressively more desperate situation at home—has increased, and NGOs [nongovernmental organizations], international organizations, and governments in neighboring countries are reporting an upsurge in these Zimbabweans facing conditions of exploitation, including human trafficking. Rural Zimbabwean men, women, and children are trafficked internally to farms for agricultural labor and domestic servitude and to cities for domestic labor and commercial sexual exploitation. Women and children are trafficked for domestic labor and sexual exploitation, including in brothels, along both sides of the borders with Botswana, Mozambique, South Africa, and Zambia. Young men and boys are trafficked to South Africa for farm work, often laboring for months in South Africa without pay before "employers" have them arrested and deported as illegal immigrants. Young women and girls are lured to South Africa, the People's Republic of China, Egypt, the United Kingdom, the United States, and Canada with false employment offers that result in involuntary domestic servitude or commercial sexual exploitation. Men, women, and children from the Democratic Republic of the Congo, Malawi, Mozambique, and Zambia are trafficked through Zimbabwe en route to South Africa. Small numbers of South African girls are trafficked to Zimbabwe for domestic servitude.

US Department of State,
"Trafficking in Persons Report," 2008.

Statistics on Human Trafficking

She added that under their regional counter-trafficking programme they have assisted about 30 Zimbabweans who were victims of trafficking.

"Under IOM's regional counter-trafficking programme, we have thus far assisted 307 victims of trafficking between January 2004 and April 2010, including 60 minors. Zimbabweans comprised some 10% of the total beneficiaries," she added.

IOM said South Africa is the main destination of trafficked victims in southern Africa. It also found trafficking in women and children for sexual exploitation to be a significant problem in southern Africa. IOM focused in part on child trafficking from Lesotho to the Eastern Free State. Victims were both male and female, with half the children abducted and half deceived. Physical and/or sexual abuse at home as well as death of a parent(s) from AIDS-related diseases were major sources of vulnerability.

Criminals Exploit Legal Loopholes

Police spokesperson, Senior Assistant Commissioner Wayne Bvudzijena, concurred with IOM's observation that tracking trafficking cases was hampered by lack of laws specifically dealing with the crime.

"We have a legislative loophole. Our laws only speak of kidnapping or abduction and are silent on trafficking in persons which is a sophisticated crime more often than not involving highly organised crime syndicates," Bvudzijena said. "Officially we have only handled one case of a Zimbabwean who was taken to Kenya under false pretences."

He added that they suspected some trafficking victims passed through the country under the guise of asylum seekers and therefore Zimbabwe had an obligation to assist them with safe passage.

"We do not have statistics of trafficked persons. We suspect other nationals may be passing through disguised as asylum seekers and under international convention on refugees, Zimbabwe cannot do anything but assist the persons," Bvudzijena added.

Zimbabweans' vulnerability has been further exacerbated by the country's decade-long economic meltdown due to political impasse among the main political rivals, Zanu-PF [Zimbabwe African National Union–Patriotic Front] and the MDC [Movement for Democratic Change] formations, lack of foreign direct investment and the general world economic recession in the last two years.

The Scope of the Problem

According to a 2009 UN's Global Initiative to Fight Human Trafficking report there are 130,000 trafficking victims in sub-Saharan Africa and most of them are between the ages of 18 and 24. Of these, 95% experience physical or sexual violence.

The report further states that 43% of the victims are used for commercial sexual exploitation and 98% of them are women and girls, while 32% are used for forced economic exploitation and woman and girls make up 56% of these. Ironically, many of the trafficked victims have at least middle level education according to the UN.

Bosnia Has a Growing Human Trafficking Crisis

Alexandra Scherle

Alexandra Scherle is a reporter for Deutsche Welle, *Germany's international broadcaster. In the following viewpoint, she identifies a new crime trend in Bosnia: organized crime going after young, vulnerable girls to force them into prostitution and pornography. Scherle reports that women's groups have been lobbying the government to take a bigger role in rehabilitating victims of the crime, but Balkan officials claim they have little money to address the problem and few resources to fight it.*

As you read, consider the following questions:

1. How does organized crime force young girls into prostitution in Bosnia, according to the viewpoint?
2. Who does Scherle say made up the victims of human trafficking in Bosnia before 2005?
3. What does women's advocate Mara Radovanovic think the government should do to help victims?

Even 12-year-old girls from good families can end up forced into prostitution in Bosnia. First the pimps spy on a girl and figure out who in her family she loves the most. Then they tell her they're going to kill that very person if she refuses to work as a prostitute for them. That's according to

Alexandra Scherle, "The Trafficking of Young Girls Booms in the Balkans," *Deutsche Welle*, December 2, 2010. Reproduced with permission.

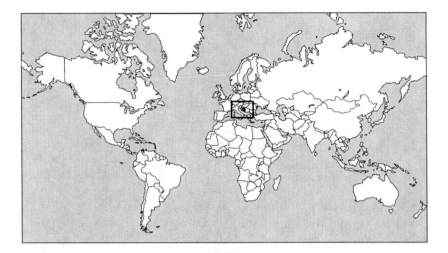

Mara Radovanovic of the women's organization LARA in Bosnia, which is now supported by the international organization
CARE. Radovanovic has established a network to fight human
trafficking and set up a women's shelter in a secret location
where she cares for victims.

High-Level Johns

Other girls are drugged and then gang raped in motels. The
perpetrators film everything and then threaten to put the
video on the Internet. The fear of public humiliation silences
the girls. Radovanovic told Deutsche Welle that even supposed
"leaders" of Bosnian society are involved in these crimes.

That was the case of one Roma girl in her shelter, who
comes from a village near the eastern town of Srebrenica. "She
was abused by teachers and the local police," Radovanovic
said. "Even the Bosnian security minister was involved."

The girl testified against the minister in the shelter, which
has directly felt the results. "In the past we got funding from
the security ministry, but since then the support has stopped,"
Radovanovic said. She said she didn't expect any more funds
as long as that particular politician is in power.

He had claimed to have met with the girl to give her a scholarship for school. Because the girl has a photographic memory, she was able to describe all the details of the minister's car to the police, thus proving that she really had been lured into his car, and not for educational purposes.

Today Bosnian border guards and police officers are better trained to identify these trafficking victims, which also reduces the number of foreign victims in the country.

A New Trend

Going after local Bosnian girls is the new trend for organized crime in the region, according to Radovanovic. Up until 2005, most of the victims were foreign girls and women who were lured from across Eastern Europe by alleged job offers in the West.

Instead of ending up working as a babysitter or waitress in Germany, however, they were then carried off to the Balkans and forced to work as prostitutes. Awareness efforts from a few brave activists have now brought this issue into the public consciousness. Today Bosnian border guards and police officers are better trained to identify these trafficking victims, which also reduces the number of foreign victims in the country.

A Risky Fight

Victims of forced prostitution and human trafficking can only be helped, Radovanovic said, if the state intervenes.

"The most important thing is to force our government to provide the resources for the rehabilitation of these victims," she said. "School scholarships for example. Because otherwise they can't be helped in the long term."

The Bosnian government has one response: There's no money available. But Radovanovic will keep fighting for the

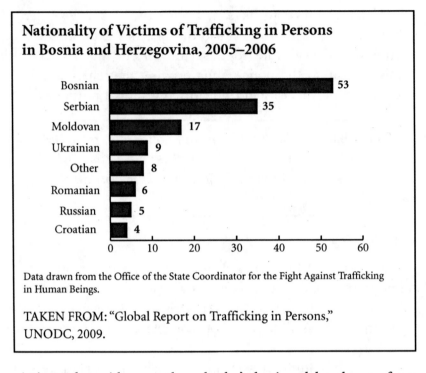

**Nationality of Victims of Trafficking in Persons
in Bosnia and Herzegovina, 2005–2006**

Nationality	Value
Bosnian	53
Serbian	35
Moldovan	17
Ukrainian	9
Other	8
Romanian	6
Russian	5
Croatian	4

Data drawn from the Office of the State Coordinator for the Fight Against Trafficking in Human Beings.

TAKEN FROM: "Global Report on Trafficking in Persons,"
UNODC, 2009.

victims, she said, even though she's besieged by threats from the Bosnian mafia and it's almost impossible to protect them.

Radovanovic's organization may have the support of European police forces and the Organization for Security and Co-operation in Europe, but she says silence is often what keeps her and her colleagues safe.

"The most important thing is the following: We know that the criminals are out there that would be very quick to kill someone," she said. "So even if we have evidence against someone, we keep this knowledge to ourselves. Knowledge is the best way for us to protect ourselves—anything else would mean certain death."

South Africa Is a Hotbed for Human Trafficking

Rebecca Wynn

Rebecca Wynn works for the International Organization for Migration's Southern African Counter-Trafficking Assistance Programme. In the following viewpoint, she examines the alarming scope of the human trafficking problem in the countries that make up southern Africa. Wynn elucidates recent efforts by the International Organization for Migration (IOM) that ensure countries in the region criminalize trafficking, effectively prosecute cases, and provide rehabilitation to victims.

As you read, consider the following questions:

1. How many people are estimated to have been trafficked across national borders every year, according to the viewpoint?
2. What are the three action points of the United Nations to combat human trafficking?
3. According to Wynn, how do current laws treat human trafficking victims in South Africa?

A cross southern Africa today men, women and children are being deceived. Struggling to survive in situations of destitution, they are promised jobs that seem to offer lifelines, but merely mark the beginning of their exploitation. These

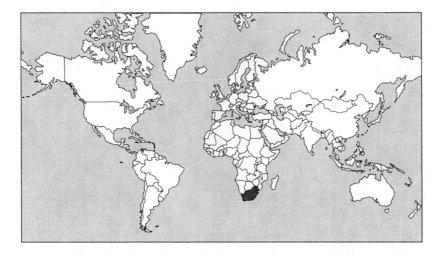

people are victims of one of the most chilling aspects of contemporary migration—human trafficking.

The Horrors of Human Trafficking

For 15-year-old Faith, the impact was devastating. Struggling to make ends meet in Bulawayo, Zimbabwe, she was approached by a man offering waitressing at a Johannesburg restaurant. But the promise was false. There was no restaurant job. Once in Johannesburg, Faith was beaten, abused, locked in a Hillbrow flat and forced into prostitution to earn profits for her traffickers.

Globally, human trafficking is considered the third-largest source of profits for organised crime with only small-weapons trafficking and drug smuggling more lucrative. It is estimated that up to one million people are trafficked across borders annually, with many more trafficked internally in their own countries.

Human trafficking is the process of recruitment and transportation of people by means of deception or force for the purpose of exploitation. This exploitation most commonly involves forced prostitution, but victims are also trafficked for bonded labour and domestic servitude. Victims can be men, women or children.

Destination: South Africa

Having conducted research on trafficking issues in the region since 2003, the International Organization for Migration's (IOM's) Southern African Counter-Trafficking Assistance Programme has found human trafficking is thriving in southern Africa, with South Africa and its expanding sex industry the main regional destination. Research also reveals that victims are trafficked from SADC [Southern African Development Community] states into South Africa, as well as from South-east Asia and Eastern Europe. IOM has also helped victims trafficked to South Africa and assisted South Africans who have been trafficked abroad, for example into forced domestic labour in Ireland and the Middle East.

Globally, human trafficking is considered the third-largest source of profits for organised crime with only small-weapons trafficking and drug smuggling more lucrative.

Globally government action on trafficking is centred on the United Nations protocol to prevent, suppress and punish trafficking in persons, and the majority of governments in the region have ratified this instrument. This has committed governments to criminalising human trafficking and developing legislation against it.

Addressing the Problem

However, translating a willingness to stamp out trafficking into effective legislation is not an easy task. To assist with this, IOM brought government officials from 13 southern African countries, as well as Comoros and Seychelles, together in Gaborone, Botswana, as a part of its Migration Dialogue for Southern Africa process this week [June 3–9, 2007]. The aim is to galvanise the counter-trafficking efforts of governments and to provide them with a forum in which to share ideas and experiences on the development of effective anti-trafficking legislation.

The Criminal Justice Response to Human Trafficking in South Africa

A Trafficking Desk was established within the Organized Crime Unit of the South African Police Service. The Sexual Offences and Community Affairs Unit belonging to the National Prosecution Service (NPS) deals with the prevention of sexual offences through effective prosecutions.

Due to the absence of legislation covering the reporting period, no prosecutions and convictions were recorded up to 2007.

United Nations Office on Drugs and Crime,
"Global Report on Trafficking in Persons," 2009.

It is crucial that trafficking is criminalised across the southern Africa region to ensure that traffickers are properly prosecuted and victims adequately protected. There are existing legal measures that can be used to prosecute traffickers, but are not sufficient to adequately punish or deter traffickers or protect victims effectively. Currently traffickers can be charged for criminal acts that happen as a part of the trafficking process, but not for trafficking itself.

Crimes such as kidnapping, abduction, rape and bringing people into the country without proper documentation, often occur as a part of the trafficking process and traffickers can be tried for these offences. However this is a blunt instrument. These acts do not necessarily have to occur for trafficking to take place. For example, trafficked Thai women arriving at OR Tambo International Airport often have all the correct documentation needed for entry to South Africa and are more commonly lured by false promises than taken by force. Defining trafficking in law as recruiting and transporting people by means of deception or force for the purpose of exploiting them means that these women's traffickers will not escape prosecution.

It is crucial that countries in the region coordinate as they develop trafficking legislation.

Protecting the Victims

Comprehensive trafficking legislation would also secure victims of trafficking more protection. Ironically under today's legal framework it is the trafficked victims who are being treated like criminals. A victim of trafficking can be arrested and prosecuted for offences committed as a direct result of him/her being trafficked.

A victim who has entered the country without documentation can be charged under the Immigration Act and a woman who has been forced into prostitution by her trafficker can presently be prosecuted for prostitution. A law that recognises trafficked persons as victims of a severe human rights abuse would change that. It would also prevent the summary deportation of trafficked victims back to the circumstances that made them vulnerable to trafficking in the first place. Under a comprehensive trafficking law, safeguards would need to be introduced to protect and rehabilitate the victim both in her destination and home country.

Human trafficking thrives, in part, because it offers human traffickers high profits with relatively low risks. Anti-trafficking legislation will help change this opportunity structure as it will add to the arsenal that law enforcement in the region can use to prosecute traffickers. It is crucial that countries in the region coordinate as they develop trafficking legislation. Trafficking by its very nature often involves the transport of victims across borders, so sharing experience and ideas across the region will ensure that all countries have harmonised legislation and are equally able to prevent human trafficking, assist the victims and prosecute human traffickers.

Israel Is a Favorite Destination for Human Traffickers

Mona Alami

Mona Alami is a reporter. In the following viewpoint, she asserts that Israel remains a favorite destination for human trafficking because of its thriving sex industry and its binding practice, which forces foreign workers into indentured labor with Israeli employers. Alami reports that law enforcement has recently discovered that Israeli women have also been victims of sexual trafficking, with several women discovered in Great Britain and Ireland working in the sex industry.

As you read, consider the following questions:

1. Where did the US State Department place Israel on its 2007 report on human trafficking?
2. What does tier 2 indicate about a country's position on human trafficking?
3. According to TFHT, how many of the estimated ten thousand prostitutes in Israel are minors?

Israel continues to be a favorite destination for the trafficking of women for the sex industry—also known as the white slave trade—and for a form of modern slavery where migrant laborers from developing countries are exploited.

The US State Department placed Israel in Tier 2 position in its 2007 "Trafficking in Persons Report." Also, an Israeli

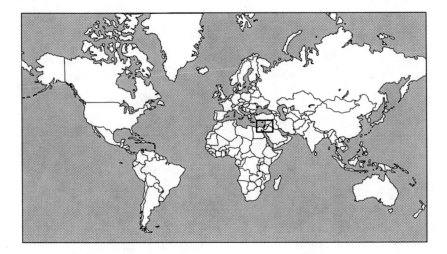

court ruled against the country's work visa policy which forces foreign workers into indentured labor with a single employer.

"Israel was only upgraded to Tier 2 last year," said Romm Lewkowicz, a spokesman from Israel's Hotline for Migrant Workers, an advocacy group which defends the rights of foreign workers.

> *In 2006, Israel was on the US State Department's Watch List for people trafficking.*

The US State Department divides countries into three tiers. Tier 1 is for countries that have successfully implemented measures to control trafficking (most Western countries fall into this category). Tier 2 is for countries that are trying to eradicate this modern-day slavery but still fail to meet the necessary standards. Tier 3 is reserved for countries that have not addressed the issue at the most basic level.

In 2006, Israel was on the US State Department's Watch List for people trafficking.

"This position falls between Tier 2 and Tier 3. The US applies economic sanctions to those countries which fall into

Tier 3, but as we have a strong economic relationship with the US, Israel was given a warning and placed in a slightly higher category," said Lewkowicz.

The Binding Work Visa Policy

The Israeli government has also faced sharp criticism from the US for its so-called binding work visa policy which effectively binds foreign migrants—mostly from developing countries and former Soviet eastern bloc countries working in certain industries such as construction, labor, home care and agriculture—to the employer stated on their visa.

"The issuance of these visas is subject to the workers staying with the same employer stated on the visa, and if this condition is broken then the migrant worker is deemed illegal and liable for deportation without having a chance to fight the case in court," said Sigal Rosen from Hotline.

This has encouraged unscrupulous employers to withhold payment and extort employees, knowing they can always replace them and escape penalized.

Turks for Tanks

One of the more notorious cases was the Turks for Tanks deal of 2002. According to the deal, the Israeli military industry (Ta'as) upgraded about 200 tanks for Turkey for US$687 million, in one of the country's biggest arms export deals. As part of the agreement, 800 Turkish workers were granted permits to work in construction in Israel, after being placed through the Turkish employment agency Yilmazlar.

One of Yilmazlar's contractors, Shaheen Yelmaz, arrived in Israel in 2006 dreaming of helping his father pay off his mounting debts after being promised a good job in Israel for $1,400 a month—a fortune by Turkey's standards where unemployment is high.

On arrival his passport and mobile phone were taken away and he and other Turkish workers were accommodated in squalid conditions.

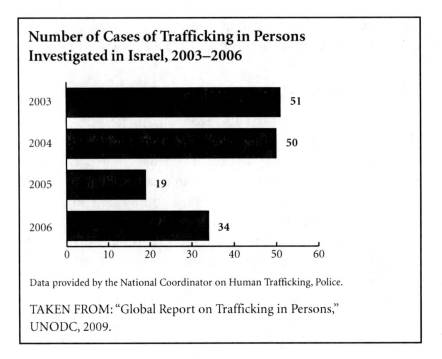

Number of Cases of Trafficking in Persons Investigated in Israel, 2003–2006

2003	51
2004	50
2005	19
2006	34

Data provided by the National Coordinator on Human Trafficking, Police.

TAKEN FROM: "Global Report on Trafficking in Persons," UNODC, 2009.

"We were not allowed to leave the premises in the evenings, and were only allowed out on our day off. And we were not paid for the first three months," said Yelmaz.

The Turkish Embassy was unwilling to intervene because of the lucrative deal with Israel.

Yelmaz and his fellow contractors, most of them with little education, were coerced into signing blank documents before leaving Turkey that virtually ensured their dependency on Yilmazlar.

"We were also told by our Israeli employer that if we were unhappy we could leave. The police would then arrest us as illegals and we would be deported," said Yelmaz.

Resolution of the Case

Following a number of similar cases, Hotline and other Israeli human rights organizations petitioned the Israeli High Court.

The court acknowledged the inequity of the system, but ruled that Yilmazlar's contract with the Israeli defense industry was unique, and the company's contract with Israel was limited.

However, the court did rule in 2006 that Israel's binding visa policy in general was illegal, and ordered the state to establish an alternative. Rosen says they are still waiting for a final response from the state.

Yelmaz was subsequently deported to Turkey, $15,000 in debt, and Israel's contract with Yilmazlar was renewed.

"While the situation of indentured laborers remains serious, the white trade trafficking has improved somewhat," said Lewkowicz. "Since the US State Department put Israel on its Watch List in 2006, the number of women trafficked to Israel has declined, and it is now against the law to traffic in women. Furthermore, the government now grants prostitutes a one-year rehabilitation visa. However, the bureaucracy involved means the granting of these visas is often problematic."

New Problems for Israel

But new problems have arisen. "Israel is no longer solely an importer of prostitutes but has become an exporter of them too. Last year [2007] we discovered a new business where Israeli women were being trafficked to the UK [United Kingdom] and Ireland to work in the sex industry," Lewkowicz said.

Prostitution has also gone underground in Israel. "Before it was openly done on the streets, now many of the players have resorted to working from private apartments, following a police and government crackdown on the trafficking," he added.

According to the Jerusalem-based Task Force on Human Trafficking (TFHT), approximately 1,000 of the estimated 10,000 prostitutes in Israel are minors.

Immigrants from the ex-Soviet bloc countries, some involved in the Russian mafia, manage about 20% of the trade, while the remainder are Israelis, says Lewkowicz.

A Global Terrorism Analysis report published by the Washington-based Jamestown Foundation states that many of the trafficked women are smuggled in from Egypt's Sinai by Bedouins who have also been involved in arms smuggling.

The industry has proved very lucrative for the human traffickers, with each woman sold in Israel bringing in anywhere between $50,000 to $100,000.

But the state also earns a tidy profit from the white slave trade, according to Hotline.

Service providers, such as taxi drivers transporting prostitutes, lawyers who represent the clients, landlords who rent out their premises as brothels, all pay income tax, and this ultimately arrives in the state's coffers. Not to mention the cases of corrupt police officers who have also lined their pockets through bribery.

Israeli Authorities Are Not Doing Enough to Reduce Human Trafficking

Dana Weiler-Polak

Dana Weiler-Polak is a reporter for Haaretz, *Israel's oldest daily newspaper. In the following viewpoint, she contends that a recent report by Israel's Knesset Research and Information Center exposes the lackluster efforts of a special Interior Ministry unit— the Oz unit— tasked with reducing human trafficking. Weiler-Polak notes that cases of human trafficking are more common and that activists are concerned that the Oz unit must take the crime more seriously.*

As you read, consider the following questions:

1. How many victims of human trafficking has the Interior Ministry unit located as of October 2009?
2. According to a 2004 estimate, what is the number of victims of human trafficking in Israel?
3. How many inspectors does the Oz unit have to investigate human trafficking cases, according to the author?

The Interior Ministry unit responsible for locating victims of human trafficking has not found a single person being trafficked for forced labor or sexual exploitation, although a 2004 government estimate put the number of victims of human trafficking between 2,000 and 3,000.

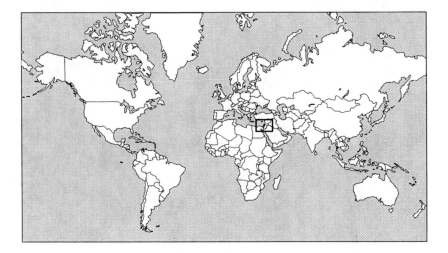

A report by the Knesset Research and Information Center, which conducts research for legislators, indicates that the ministry's Oz unit is the government body responsible for reducing human trafficking. But the authorities are not doing enough to reduce "modern-day slavery," said Hanny Ben-Israel, a lawyer for the workers advocacy group Kav La'Oved.

"Treatment of the matter is insufficient, due primarily to a lack of awareness that this is a serious criminal offense," she said. "A failure to locate victims shows only that the unit is disconnected from what's happening on the ground, and when someone doesn't know what he's supposed to be looking for, it's no surprise that he doesn't find it."

Since the Oz unit was founded four months ago, to replace the Interior Ministry's Immigration Administration, it has not provided police with any information that could lead to a criminal investigation, making it difficult for the law enforcement authorities to bring to justice those responsible for human trafficking.

However, things may begin to change shortly. Starting next week, Oz unit members are scheduled to undergo training in how to identify victims of trafficking.

For now, though, the unit may be ignoring human trafficking even when its inspectors do come across it.

"It's not just that they didn't find anyone, but that they even ignored a clear case of trafficking when they raided an escort service, arrested the women and deported them to Moldova," said Yonatan Berman, a lawyer for the advocacy group Hotline for Migrant Workers. "We offered to give the unit workshops on this issue, but we haven't received any response."

Since the Oz unit was founded four months ago [June 2009], to replace the Interior Ministry's Immigration Administration, it has not provided police with any information that could lead to a criminal investigation.

Berman said his group alone receives dozens of complaints concerning human trafficking every year, adding, "It's clear that the situation is actually a lot worse than that."

Indeed, the numbers may be on the rise.

Ben-Israel said Kav La'Oved has recently been receiving more complaints than usual about human trafficking, which includes forced prostitution or sexual exploitation as well as what the U.S. State Department describes as "forced labor, including the unlawful withholding of passports, restrictions on movement, non-payment of wages, threats, and physical intimidation."

"We have recently encountered an uptick in complaints on the matter," she said. "It's a serious phenomenon, especially in agriculture. We recently dealt with a series of serious incidents involving laborers who were working 18 hours a day, their passports were taken from them, they were threatened, they worked without protection—really modern-day slavery."

This year's State Department report on human trafficking classified Israel as a country whose government does not fully comply with the minimum standards required to eliminate human trafficking, but is "making significant efforts" to comply with those standards.

"Israel is a destination country for men and women trafficked for the purposes of forced labor and sexual exploitation," the report says. "Low-skilled workers from China, Romania, Turkey, Thailand, the Philippines, Nepal, Sri Lanka, and India migrate voluntarily and legally to Israel for contract labor in the construction, agriculture, and health care industries. . . . Women from Russia, Ukraine, Moldova, Uzbekistan, Belarus, and China are trafficked to Israel for forced prostitution, often by organized crime groups across the border with Egypt."

The report recommends that Israel significantly increase "prosecutions, convictions, and sentences for forced labor offenses, including the unlawful practice of withholding passports as a means to keep a person in a form of labor or service; increase investigations, prosecutions, and punishments of internal trafficking for commercial sexual exploitation; and extend comprehensive protection services to victims of forced labor."

While the Oz unit has 160 inspectors and a NIS 50 million annual budget, it has "focused solely on locating illegal aliens and dealing with them," said MK Orit Zuaretz (Kadima), who heads the Knesset subcommittee on trafficking in women.

"Even though the unit was supposed to replace the Immigration Administration, including in everything related to locating and identifying trafficking victims, that hasn't been done," said Zuaretz.

"Law enforcement in the field of fighting human trafficking requires the active inspection of employers," said Kav La'Oved lawyer Anat Kidron. "Such inspection is not being done to a sufficient extent, and therefore a significant number of the victims of trafficking are not being found."

Periodical and Internet Sources Bibliography

The following articles have been selected to supplement the diverse views presented in this chapter.

Matthew Chance   "Russia's Sex Slave Industry Thrives, Rights Groups Say," CNN, July 18, 2008. http://articles.cnn.com.

Cassandra Clifford   "Global Human Trafficking Report Shows the Even Darker Side," *Global Posts* (blog), March 3, 2009. http://children.foreigpolicyblogs.com.

CNN   "Human Trafficking in Mexico Targets Women and Children," January 13, 2010. http://articles.cnn.com.

Youngbee Dale   "Russia's Political Ambition Leaves the Human Victims Behind," Examiner.com, June 1, 2010. www.examiner.com.

Nthambeleni Gabara   "Human Trafficking Plagues Country," *BuaNews* (Tshwane, South Africa), March 24, 2010.

Steven Gigliotti   "Human Trafficking in the US, a Growing Problem," *Epoch Times*, November 23, 2010.

Emilio Godoy   "Five Million Women Have Fallen Prey to Trafficking Networks," Inter Press Service, September 22, 2010. http://ipsnews.net.

Mickey Goodman   "Sex Trafficking in the United States: Children Across America Are Unseen Victims," *Huffington Post*, January 23, 2011. www.huffingtonpost.com.

Erika Klein   "Human Sex Trafficking: Canada's Hidden Crime," The Mantle, February 24, 2010. http://mantlethought.org.

Natalie Simpson   "Human Trafficking: Australia's Sinister Practice," *Liberty News*, Winter 2010.

GLOBALVIEWPOINTS

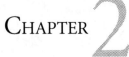

CHAPTER 2

Factors Contributing to Human Trafficking

Global Human Trafficking Is a By-Product of Capitalism

Julia Suryakusuma

Julia Suryakusuma is an author and commentator. In the following viewpoint, she argues that human trafficking and sex work thrive because there is a lucrative market for both. Suryakusuma contends that authorities should continue to combat human trafficking and forced prostitution, but should ease up on individuals who freely choose to engage in sex work.

As you read, consider the following questions:

1. What does Nori Andriyani assert in her book *Jakarta Uncovered*?
2. What is GAYa Nusantara's stance on prostitution, according to the author?
3. From where do Elizabeth Pisani's insights in her book *The Wisdom of Whores* come?

S ex sells.

Nobody knows that better than prostitutes, or "sex workers", as the politically correct call them these days. But you can only sell if there are buyers: supply and demand, the simple logic of our capitalist world.

In a recently published book, *Jakarta Uncovered: Exposing Immorality, Building a New Consciousness*, Nori Andriyani—

feminist and NGO [nongovernmental organization] activist, lecturer, and former journalist—questions why is it always the woman, the sex worker, who is blamed for the oldest profession's activities? In Indonesia they used to be called WTS, which stands for wanita tuna susila—woman without morals. Like many in the past, Nori asks what about the men who do the purchasing? Shouldn't they be called PTS, pria tuna susila—men without morals?

A Question of Morality

Is morality really the issue? While no doubt full of good intentions, the stance that Nori takes is typical of books about prostitution in Indonesia. Even Moammar Emka's best-selling *Jakarta Undercover*, adopts the same voyeuristic-cum-moralistic tone.

At least Nori makes no bones about the fact that her concern about the sex industry derives from her position as a wife and mother. She fears she might one day go through what her best friend "Siti" did, discovering that her husband habitually bought sex.

Nori prefers to call "the oldest profession" the "oldest oppression" in the world. She argues that the immorality of prostitution is often forced on women, who invariably do it because of economic need. This sounds convincing, but unfortunately it's not always true. Some sex workers actually derive sexual pleasure from their clients.

Those who can afford to be selective will choose the ones they like. Some have a regular clientele and even develop "relationships" with their customers.

Wealthy housewives have also been known to "moonlight" as prostitutes just for kicks, because they're bored, or maybe to get even with their sex-marauding husbands. What's good for the goose is good for the gander, after all.

And there's even the case of a sex worker who got married to a much older man, but missed the days when she was "on

---

The Sex Trafficking Trap

Sex trafficking comprises a smaller but still significant portion of overall human trafficking. When an adult is coerced, forced, or deceived into prostitution—or maintained in prostitution through coercion—that person is a victim of trafficking. All of those involved in recruiting, transporting, harboring, receiving, or obtaining the person for that purpose have committed a trafficking crime. Sex trafficking can also occur within debt bondage, as women and girls are forced to continue in prostitution through the use of unlawful "debt" purportedly incurred through their transportation, recruitment, or even their crude "sale"—which exploiters insist they must pay off before they can be free. It is critical to understand that a person's initial consent to participate in prostitution is not legally determinative: If they are thereafter held in service through psychological manipulation or physical force, they are trafficking victims and should receive the benefits outlined in the Palermo Protocol [also known as the United Nations Protocol to Prevent, Suppress and Punish Trafficking in Persons, Especially Women and Children] and applicable domestic laws.

US Department of State
"Trafficking in Persons Report," June 2010.

---

the make" and could still experience the big "O". Her husband was only interested in his own pleasure, but she put up with it for the sake of the economic security of her two kids. Isn't this in its own way a kind of prostitution, selling your soul, spirit and pleasure for money? At least prostitutes only sell their bodies. As Angela Carter said: "What is marriage but prostitution to one man instead of many?"

The Facts of Life

Personally, I'm not that interested in the morality issues when it comes to the sex trade. Prostitution, trafficking and pornography are all facts of life, and have been around from time immemorial.

They are certainly part and parcel of capitalism, politics, militarism, and human beings' fundamental physical urges. No amount of "consciousness raising" or education in gender equality can eradicate it. The proof? The increased proliferation of the sex industry in Jakarta for the "haves", safely ensconced in five-star hotels, immune to police raids that the sex workers constantly fight off, sometimes at the cost of their lives.

Prostitution, trafficking and pornography are all facts of life, and have been around from time immemorial.

If for the lower classes it's to do with economic need, and fraught with damned-if-you-do, damned-if-you-don't choices, how can they afford to be moralistic? Nurhayati, a divorcee in *At Stake* (2007), the omnibus produced by Nia Dinata, works as a stone crusher by day.

It is impossible not to be touched as she lovingly tucks her two small children in bed, kisses them goodnight and then goes off to her night job as a sex worker in Bolo cemetery in Tulungagung, East Java. How else can she afford to feed and clothe her kids and send them to school?

Keeping Trafficking a Crime

That's why I prefer the (unofficial) position on prostitution adopted by GAYa Nusantara, the oldest LGBT [lesbian, gay, bisexual, transgender] organization in Indonesia. They believe that people have the right to sell sex, that sex workers shouldn't be stigmatized but regarded as workers, and that they have the right to organize. Prostitution, they say, should be decriminalized and regulated with a view to protecting sex workers from abuse. (They do, however, regard forced prostitution and trafficking as crimes.)

I also like Elizabeth Pisani's *The Wisdom of Whores*, although the title is a bit of a teaser, because the book is really about policies in the AIDS industry. She talks about what's gone wrong in the fight against the millennial plague, about why the public health system has lost our trust and why governments waste billions of dollars on the wrong policies. But where do her insights come from? Besides drug users, sex workers, of course.

What about the prostitutes in politics, in the government, legislature and judiciary? . . . I'd be more inclined to impose standards of morality on them.

On World AIDS Day last week, the *Jakarta Post* published an article titled "Sex workers at the forefront of disease prevention" (Dec. 1, 2010). In fact they are champions of safe sex, encouraging their clients to use condoms, sometimes at the risk of physical abuse. Even the establishments they work in put up stickers in each room promoting safe sex. Well, restaurants have an interest in keeping their kitchens clean, so why not brothels?

Anyway, what about the prostitutes in politics, in the government, legislature and judiciary? You know, the ones who put our nation's future up for sale? Personally, I'd be more inclined to impose standards of morality on them. Ethics, it's called. Wonder if they've ever heard of it?

Nepal's Human Trafficking Problem Is a Result of Poverty

Barbara Gunnell

Barbara Gunnell is a writer and editor. In the following view-point, she asserts that Nepal's failing economy has resulted in a rise in the sex trafficking of young women and girls, often forced into brothels in foreign cities. Gunnell argues that with many of Nepal's young people eager to leave their impoverished country and find work elsewhere, women are particularly vulnerable to unscrupulous employment agencies and shady acquaintances who will sell them into servitude. She urges British citizens to acknowledge the problem and recognize their attitudes toward migrants in general.

As you read, consider the following questions:

1. According to the United Nations Protocol to Prevent, Suppress and Punish Trafficking in Persons, Especially Women and Children, what is the difference between trafficking victims and "consenting migrants"?

2. According to the International Labour Organization, how many women and children are trafficked every year from Nepal?

3. What does Gunnell assert are the annual profits from human trafficking?

Barbara Gunnell, "Nothing to Sell but Their Bodies," *New Statesman*, March 1, 2004. Reproduced by permission.

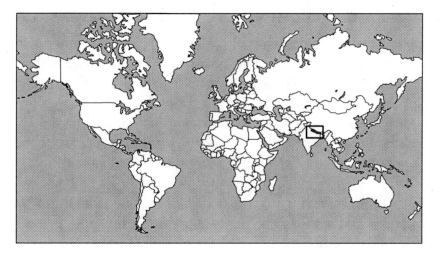

"Do you have people-trafficking in Britain?" Ambika Acharya asked. We were in Melamchi village in Sindhupalchok, a district of eastern Nepal considered particularly vulnerable to trafficking of women and girls for prostitution. Neither of us knew it until the following day but, as she was posing the question, the tragedy of the Chinese cocklepickers was unfolding in Morecambe.

I answered Acharya's question with a story, published in the *New Statesman* last August [2003], about Chinese labourers working on farms in Norfolk. They were bound to their gangmasters by the debts they had incurred for their illegal passage to England. If they failed to repay the debts in full, reprisals would be taken against their families back in China.

Acharya and the other members of Mank, Melamchi's anti-trafficking group, would have identified with almost every element of the Chinese migrant workers' tale, from the slave-labour conditions to the bondage of debt and the threat to families. The group campaigns in a region with a history of forced prostitution, one where, even a few decades ago, ruling families exercised droit du seigneur [feudal law] over local girls.

Modern-Day Slavery

Today, instead, girls as young as ten are kidnapped and taken across the border to be sold to brothels in India. Often their families are complicit. Money may be paid to the family. The brothel will pay the trafficker. The girl will have to earn—with interest—the money the brothel paid for her before she receives anything herself. Sometimes girls who manage to escape report that even after several years the debt remained undischarged.

A common story is for a girl or young woman to be drugged and abducted to the brothels of Kathmandu, or over the Indian border to those of Delhi and Mumbai. Survivors speak of waking from a stupor to find themselves sold into prostitution.

Rita Tamang (a pseudonym she chose herself) tells a typical tale. Nine years ago, she was abducted and imprisoned for some months in a brothel in Mumbai.

"My family is Nepalese, but we went to live in Himachal Pradesh in India when I was five," Tamang tells me in a halting voice. "We ran out of money and moved to Nainital, where my father got work. There, one of his friends tried to convince me to go with him to work somewhere else. I was 17 and said no; I didn't want to leave my parents. Then this person gave me some sweets. I woke up in a brothel but I didn't know that's what it was. I asked the woman in charge what work I had to do: 'Is it washing clothes?' I asked.

"They told me I had to do this sex work, and threatened me with a knife. I wouldn't, so they moved me to another brothel and this time I did. I was there six months and then the Indian government raided us. I was taken by the police to a place called Chempur, which was like a jail. We were there, 150 of us in one room, for seven months, without beds, and no contact with outside. The Indians said they had asked the Nepal government to take us back but it wouldn't. Finally, some charities heard about us and we were split into seven different houses. Those in my house started the organization Shakti Samuha [now a campaigning group for survivors, working with Oxfam] to help others like us."

Tamang, now free and married (unusually: there is great prejudice against women who have been trafficked), has never found her family. Wasn't she angry with her relatives for failing to protect her from the family "friend"? No, she was convinced that her father knew nothing of what happened.

Deceived into Prostitution

Other women tell of being deceived by "manpower agencies" that promise lucrative domestic or factory jobs in the Gulf or Hong Kong. Yet others, though it can never be admitted, may find the prospect of working in India's squalid brothels more appealing than an impoverished future in Nepal's failed economy, where more than half the population lives below the poverty line and almost half is out of work for at least part of the year. Nepal spends three times as much each year trying to extinguish the eight-year Maoist [Communist] insurgency as it spends on education, with the result that only 42 per cent of women and 62 per cent of men have any reading and writing skills.

The UN [United Nations] Protocol to Prevent, Suppress and Punish Trafficking in Persons, Especially Women and Children (2000) distinguishes between those abducted—for example to work in Indian brothels, or children sold to embroidery sweatshops, circus owners and camel racers—and the self-chosen hardships of illegal immigrants. Unicef [the United Nations Children's Fund] puts it thus: "The smuggling of migrants, while often undertaken in dangerous or degrading conditions, involves migrants who have consented to the smuggling. Trafficking victims, on the other hand, have either never consented or, if they initially consented, that consent has been rendered meaningless by the coercive, deceptive or abusive actions of the traffickers."

HIV and Trafficking Victims

The sad fact is despite such well-known institutions and others such as Human Rights Watch which has chronicled the legal and human rights violations in the act, Nepalese girls continue being trafficked and sold for prostitution in India. The victims are only abandoned when they become infected with HIV. For instance, of 218 Nepalese girls rescued in February 1996 from a Bombay police raid, 60–70% of them were HIV positive.

Surya B. Prasai, "Call for Global Action to Halt Nepalese Women and Girls Trafficking," American Chronicle, *February 10, 2008.*

But the stories of those who are deceived into prostitution are barely distinguishable from stories of "consenting migrants" who are deceived into paying their passage to a country and a job, but find instead that they are bonded labour.

Questioning Consent

There are other reasons to be wary of watertight definitions. In Nepal, women's right to migrate in search of a better life has been severely curtailed by the conflation of trafficking and prostitution: the best-funded anti-trafficking charity in Nepal appears to hold that a woman (like a child) cannot consent to prostitution. Thus, any woman crossing the border may be expected to prove that she isn't being trafficked. I spoke to women applying for passports at the Sindhupalchok district offices in Chautara. As well as requiring the permission of a parent or guardian, women, unlike men, are interviewed about their intentions and counselled about the dangers they might face. Well-meaning it may be, but the implication is that a woman with a passport must be in search of a brothel.

The conflation of prostitution with trafficking also infects major programmes in Nepal. The United States labour department funds the International Labour Organization's [ILO's] anti-trafficking programme and will not allow the ILO to use the term "sex work", so Anders Lisborg, an expert on trafficking, chooses his words carefully. The framework of "search and rescue" and the belief that every cross-border bus contains kidnapped women and children destined for Indian brothels is hampering their work, he explains. "Women have a right to the same labour mobility as men. Trafficking is not often about taking someone by force from their village. The main contribution to trafficking is dysfunctional families; alcohol is also a huge problem. Our emphasis has to shift now from interception to prevention and protection."

In Nepal, women's right to migrate in search of a better life has been severely curtailed ... the best-funded anti-trafficking charity in Nepal appears to hold that a woman cannot consent to prostitution.

The ILO is also wary of statistics on trafficking. It suggests that approximately 12,000 women and children are trafficked every year from Nepal but accepts that the figure could be higher. As India is the main destination, and shares a 1,747km [kilometre] open border with Nepal, it would be unrealistic to look for a precise figure.

A Hugely Profitable Business

Yet however one defines trafficking, the desperate and the naive all have to survive in the same shark-infested waters. Human trafficking attracts annual profits of between roughly $5bn [billion] and $7bn and is the third-biggest illegal trade after drug smuggling and gun running. So it is hardly surprising that, like them, it operates with near impunity. From

Morecambe to Melamchi, the big guns behind the lucrative racket never get caught. Occasionally the middlemen do.

Around the world, remittances from migrant workers—both men and women, and certainly including earnings from prostitution—are the mainstay of economies that have been pauperised and abandoned by the rich world. Nepal's central bank reports receipts of $1bn a year from expatriate earnings, though official estimates necessarily do not include informal ways of repatriating money. Some Nepalese economists claim that the repatriation of earnings from non-resident Nepalis now contributes more foreign exchange to the economy than development aid, which itself contributes more than any local industry, including tourism.

We prefer not to look too closely at the despair that drives people to be insulted and exploited in foreign lands, nor at the dehumanising poverty that pushes women and children into the dangers of prostitution.

We prefer not to look too closely at the despair that drives people to be insulted and exploited in foreign lands, nor at the dehumanising poverty that pushes women and children into the dangers of prostitution.

The Situation in Britain

Instead, in Britain, we obsess about asylum-seekers and would-be immigrants. We rarely think about the migrant workers already here, their rights, our obligations. They occupy the time and space that we, the legitimate, don't use (the small hours, the backstreets, the hotel basements), but now and then an event such as Morecambe forces us to acknowledge the world we are shaping. We in Europe might like to believe we are having a civilised debate about how many lucky migrants will be allowed to catch crumbs from the rich man's table this year. Meanwhile, Morecambe has shown that we are home to some of the worst abuses from trafficking in human beings. The CIA [Central Intelligence Agency] estimates that in the US there are between 45,000 and 50,000 enslaved women and children, taken there under false pretences and forced to work as prostitutes or servants.

The answer to Acharya's question is: "Yes, we do have trafficking." But unlike poverty-stricken Nepal, we prefer not to do anything about it.

China's Widespread Child Trafficking Is Aided by Corruption

Andreas Lorenz

Andreas Lorenz is a reporter for Der Spiegel. *In the following viewpoint, he investigates the widespread problem of human trafficking in China, particularly the abduction and selling of children. Lorenz reports that the difficulty of tracking and recovering the hundreds of thousands of trafficked women, children, and adolescents is exacerbated by corruption and police passivity. Lorenz finds that desperate parents are often forced to act on their own to find their abducted children.*

As you read, consider the following questions:

1. According to Lorenz, how many babies, children, and adolescents disappear every year in China?
2. How many abducted children did the Chinese police manage to rescue in 2009, according to the viewpoint?
3. How many children does the author assert disappeared in Dongguan, China, between 2008 and 2009?

G uo Gangtang sells dried pumpkin gourds in Beijing's Yiwu City shopping center. The yellow containers are imprinted with historic figures, fairies or aphorisms—designs his wife finds on the Internet.

Andreas Lorenz, "China's Child-Trafficking Epidemic," *Spiegel Online*, May 21, 2010. Reproduced by permission.

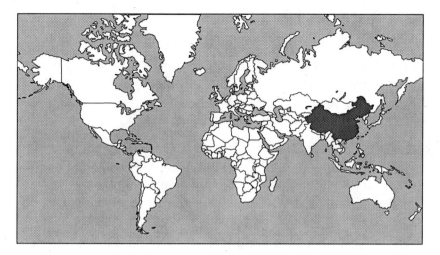

Business isn't going particularly well, partly because his stand is tucked away in a back corner, where the rent is cheaper. Guo rarely earns more than 1000 yuan (about €120 or $149) a month.

Out of pity, the landlord recently waived his rent. Fate has not treated Guo kindly. His child was stolen 13 years ago, and since then he has been motivated by only one desire: to find his son.

Whenever Guo, who is in his 40s, has saved enough money, he attaches two flags to the back seat of his moped and drives out into the countryside. The flags show a picture of a small boy, his son Xinzhen.

The day the world fell apart for Guo and his wife began like any other. He was living in a village in coastal Shandong Province, where he worked as a driver, transporting building materials on a tractor. It was Sept. 21, 1997. His little son Xinzhen, who was two-and-a-half years old, was playing with a girl from the neighborhood in front of the house door when a woman approached the children. The woman, a stranger, stroked the boy's face with a piece of cloth, eyewitnesses later reported. Then she turned slowly toward the street, which was about 100 meters (328 feet) away.

Guo Discovers His Son Gone

The little boy must have followed her. It was as if he had vanished into thin air. "When I came home, there was a crowd in front of my house," Guo recalls. "I immediately suspected that something had happened to Xinzhen."

Guo ran to the police station. Neighbors helped him to look for his little boy. He and his wife spent a lot of money during the next few weeks. They posted placards on lampposts, had flyers printed and paid helpers the equivalent of about one euro a day to search for the child in the surrounding towns.

Guo soon began searching farther afield. "I was in every province, except Tibet, Taiwan, Qinghai and Inner Mongolia," he says. Newspapers and television stations picked up the story and reported on his misfortune.

Stealing children is a common problem in the People's Republic [of China], which explains why grandparents or parents pick up children from school throughout the country. They are determined not to make it any easier for the human traffickers.

It's one of the saddest aspects of modern China. Experts estimate that between 30,000 and 60,000 babies, children and adolescents disappear each year. They are kidnapped and then sold, often ending up as slaves in workshops and brickworks, or being forced to work in brothels.

Trafficking Is Tradition

On the way to the buyer, the human traffickers often sedate the kidnapped children to prevent them from screaming. Sometimes they don't survive their ordeal, as evidenced by periodic media reports of dead children found on buses or trains.

On Nov. 30, 2008, 11 years after the disappearance of Xinzhen, two-year-old Baotong was playing in an alley in front of his parents' building in the coastal city of Lianyungang. His father, Li Shouquan, made athletic shoes in his small factory and sold them in the hallway of his apartment building.

There was a crowd of customers in the courtyard that day. A man who had been lurking unnoticed near the wall suddenly grabbed the little boy and left, leaving behind nothing but a few cigarette butts under a tiny tree.

Li suspected that his son was somewhere in neighboring Shandong Province. "There is a children's market in the town of Tanshan," a policeman told him. When he began looking around in one of the nearby villages, residents mistook him for a human trafficker. "They asked me whether I had a child to sell and how much I wanted for it," he reports. "In their eyes, human trafficking is not criminal, but is in fact part of a tradition in China."

Many Chinese desperately want a baby but are unable to conceive a child of their own.

The Cost for a Child

Sons are particularly important in the villages. It has long been a tradition in rural areas for male offspring and daughters-in-law to care for elderly parents.

But buyers for stolen children can also be found in cities like Beijing or Shanghai. Many Chinese desperately want a baby but are unable to conceive a child of their own. Adoptions are complicated, and most of the children now being handed over to orphanages are disabled.

Beijing's one-child policy doesn't impede the business. On the contrary, families that already have one child sometimes buy another son or daughter. It is lucrative business for the kidnappers, who can charge up to €4,000 for a boy and usually about half as much for a girl. They sometimes even offer special deals to less affluent customers, selling babies for as little as €80.

The police have created a special force to combat the kidnapping of children and women, and the unit breaks up human trafficking rings every year. But according to official statistics, in 2009 the police only managed to rescue 3,400 children from the clutches of dealers and buyers. In many places, a child is only considered missing after 24 hours. By then, the kidnappers are usually long gone.

Corruption Makes Trafficking Possible

Desperate parents repeatedly stage protests against police passivity. One such protest was held in the southern migrant worker city of Dongguan, where about 1,000 children disappeared between 2008 and 2009. The local police only listed 200 victims in their files. They rejected the remaining cases, claiming that there was no proof that a crime had been committed.

The chances of tracking down an abducted child are miniscule. Family clans often control things in the villages, and "they are as thick as thieves," says shoemaker Li. Local officials are part of the system, including the representatives of women's organizations, party leaders and local police officers. "Everyone knows when a new child has suddenly arrived in the village," says Li, "and no one asks any questions."

It is not just unscrupulous gangs that engage in human trafficking, as one might expect, but sometimes the parents themselves.

And then there is the corruption, China's fundamental flaw, without which human trafficking on such a large scale would not be possible. When things are done according to the rules, every child has to be registered with the relevant authorities, something which should not in fact be possible without a birth certificate and other documents. But with the right connections and a handsome bribe for officials, this hurdle is easily surmounted.

It is not just unscrupulous gangs that engage in human trafficking, as one might expect, but sometimes the parents themselves. Some farmers are so poor that they cannot or are unwilling to feed another mouth, and so they sell their newborns instead. Others view giving birth to and selling additional children as a source of income—and more lucrative than toiling in the fields. There is a saying among farmers in the southwestern province of Yunnan: "If you want to make money, you should bear children instead of raising pigs."

Buying Children Is Not a Crime

In Lushan, 300 kilometers (188 miles) west of Lianyungang, Mr. Wang is sitting on an imitation leather sofa. An attractive young man, he works as a middle school mathematics teacher. He is currently assigned to a village school in the mountains. He and his wife, who is also a teacher, admit that they bought a child.

The teacher doesn't want to provide his real name. His family, which is gathered around him, is suspicious of journalists. Under Chinese law, however, what Mr. Wang has done is not a crime. Only those who sell people can be charged with a crime, but not those who buy them.

Nevertheless, the case casts him in a bad light, as an educator who is supposed to serve as a role model for society. Mr. Wang decides to speak. He wants to demonstrate that he too is a victim. "After we had our boy, we wanted a second child," he says. "We love children. And when the opportunity presented itself, we seized it."

That opportunity arose at the People's Hospital across the main street. A relative had heard that a mother wanted to sell her newborn, because she was too poor to feed the child. At the appointed time, Mr. Wang met a man on the steps of the hospital who the teacher believed was the father. The man was holding the baby in his arms. "We gave him more than 10,000 yuan (around €1,200)," says Wang.

The baby was tiny and scrawny, but the new parents used powdered milk to help the child put on weight. "There were times when we thought the baby wouldn't make it," says the teacher's mother.

The Children Are the Victims

An album of pictures from the baby's first birthday party is on the coffee table. She looks like a happy little girl, wearing a little sun hat in one photo and sunglasses in another, or holding a mobile phone in her hand.

But the family's newfound happiness was short-lived. One day, officers turned up at the door. They were railroad police from the southwestern province of Guizhou. A few days earlier, they had noticed two suspicious-looking men traveling with three tiny children on a train to Beijing. One of them confessed to having sold a baby to Wang, the teacher. The wife of the baby dealer apparently worked as a nurse in the Lushan hospital and set up the deal.

> To improve the chances of mothers and fathers finding their children, private groups have now set up websites that allow parents to search for the missing children.

The railroad police officers took the baby girl away from the Wangs and took her to an orphanage in Guizhou. Because there was no information on the identity and whereabouts of the little girl's birth mother, she has been living in the orphanage since last September [2009].

The teacher calls it scandalous, saying that he would like to keep the girl until the real parents can be found. "I once visited the child in the orphanage. It was terrible. She didn't recognize me anymore. She has regressed, and now she no longer speaks."

Most kidnapped children who are found—or who set out to find their real parents—suffer fates similar to that of the Wangs' purchased daughter. Rarely do the police manage to find the real parents. Last year, when the police published photos of 60 rescued children on a website, only seven of their relatives came forward.

Meanwhile, more than 230 laboratories throughout the country have analyzed the DNA of parents and rescued children. The government pays the cost of the testing, about €200 per test. More than 20,000 samples have already been collected—too few to be able to effectively reunite families in such an enormous country.

As a result, many people never learn that the people who raised them are not their biological parents. To improve the chances of mothers and fathers finding their children, private groups have now set up websites that allow parents to search for the missing children.

Playing Cards with Photos of the Missing

The sound of Kenny G playing the Frank Sinatra classic "I Did It My Way" on the clarinet emerges from the loudspeakers in the main train station of Chongqing, a city on the Yangtze River in central China. A dozen people, most of them young, are holding up a banner for travelers to see. It reads: "Joint Campaign of Volunteers from Chongqing to Find Family Members."

Shen Hao, 41, a computer specialist from Anhui Province, initiated the campaign. Nine years ago, he decided to dedicate himself to the plight of the missing, when he read a newspaper story about three girls who had disappeared. Since then, he has been traveling through China's big cities, handing out playing cards with photos of the missing to passersby.

The Queen of Hearts card, for example, depicts Wang Yafeng, born April 20, 1987, in Inner Mongolia. She has been missing since Oct. 7, 2008. According to the tiny Chinese characters on the card, she has a "large nose" and "a scar on the index finger of the right hand," and "she speaks dialect-free Chinese."

The Nine of Spades features a blurred image of a young man who was born "around 1984." He is searching for his biological parents. "Kidnapped between May and September 1990," he writes. He describes himself as a child with "large eyes and a small nose," and notes that he is now 1.76 meters (5'9") tall and wears a size 41 shoe.

He writes that, as far as he can remember, he is from a city, perhaps in Hunan Province, or possibly Chongqing. "There were markets on both sides of the street. My parents wore uniforms." He remembers that strangers took him to the coastal province of Fujian on a bus.

The cards also offer tips on how to make it more difficult for traffickers to steal children. One of the recommendations is to "always keep the children in your sight." Another one is to have one's children tattooed so that they can be identified more easily later on.

"About 800 people were able to find their relatives with the help of our website and the cards," activist Shen says proudly. He has already printed 16,000 of the playing cards. He is wearing a green parka and has spiky hair. A woman who has just approached him says that she has been missing her 13-year-old son for several days. Unless he turns up soon, the boy will appear in the next batch of Shen's cards.

Support Is Hard to Come By

Shen, who receives no money from the government, pays for his campaign with his own funds, contributions from the families and company donations. Official China mistrusts nonprofit organizations like his. Nevertheless, it does provide him with assistants during his trips around the country. "Child abduction," says Shen, "is a worldwide problem. It's an extremely profitable business, like the drug trade."

It is early May, and gourd seller Guo is driving his red "Haojue" motorcycle along Highway 106 in Hubei Province, heading for Wuhan, a major city on the Yangtze River. His silver helmet, jeans, cloth shoes and knee pads are enveloped in the clouds of dust stirred up by trucks, and his chin is covered with stubble. He has covered 4,000 kilometers within the last two weeks. "I want to go to towns where I haven't been yet," he says.

When he stops to take a break at a small roadside restaurant, a few local residents stare at the flags on his moped. "My child was kidnapped," Guo explains. When he meets people with the same fate, he tells them about his experiences. "There is a police website," he says, "and you can take a DNA test."

He recently saw a picture of a ragged street urchin in a newspaper. The boy seemed to resemble his son. He quickly drove to the town, but the boy wasn't his. Guo and his wife now have two other sons, who are 12 and three years old.

What if he were to find Xinzhen after these years, possibly in an intact family? "I wouldn't force him to come back to us," says Guo. "I would just want to know that he's doing well."

Spain's Casual Acceptance of Prostitution Leads to Human Trafficking

Alasdair Fotheringham

Alasdair Fotheringham is a journalist. In the following viewpoint, he elucidates the sociohistorical reasons for the pervasive popularity and social acceptance of prostitution in Spain. Fotheringham also examines the seedy underbelly of prostitution, reporting that many of the women working in the business are victims of sex traffickers and have few legal rights.

As you read, consider the following questions:

1. What percentage of Spanish men does the United Nations say have used a prostitute's services at least once?
2. How many estimated prostitutes are working in Spain?
3. According to the Spanish newspaper *El País*, how many cases of women sold into sexual slavery were identified by authorities between January and April 2010?

The Spanish economy may be dangerously close to meltdown this week [late 2010] but one area at least—prostitution—appears to be doing very nicely, thank you.

"Don Jose—cleanliness; Don Jose—discretion; Don Jose—security, and a patrolled car park," half-whispers the calm fe-

Alasdair Fotheringham, "Spain, the World Capital of Prostitution?," *The Independent*, December 5, 2010. Reproduced with permission. www.independent.co.uk.

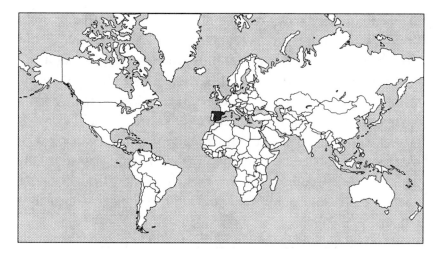

male voice on a Granada radio station throughout the day. It is an advertisement for the city's biggest and best-known brothel.

Cut to a Saturday night inside the said Don Jose "club"—three storeys high, flashing neon lights, two bars, a VIP zone and some 70 sex workers, clad in everything from nightgowns to G-strings to the very briefest of shorts—and, according to local regulars, business is booming. "The place is heaving every weekend," comments "Alvaro", an experienced brothel-goer in his late forties. "These days in the afternoons and early evenings, you'll get businessmen who've told their wives they're at meetings. Then later on, there are hordes of 18- or 19-year-olds, just there to have a laugh and, if they want, have a quick lay as well."

The Popularity of Prostitution in Spain

This is no exaggeration. Prostitution is so popular (and socially accepted) in Spain that a United Nations [UN] study reports that 39 per cent of all Spanish men have used a prostitute's services at least once. A Spanish Health Ministry survey in 2009 put the percentage of one-time prostitute users at 32 per cent: lower than the UN figure, perhaps, but far higher than the 14 per cent in liberal-minded Holland, or in Britain, where the figure is reported to oscillate between 5 and 10 per cent. And that was just those men willing to admit it.

To meet this vast demand, an estimated 300,000 prostitutes are working in Spain—everywhere from clubs in town centres to industrial estates, to lonely country roads to roadside bars, the last often recognisable by gigantic neon signs of champagne bottles or shapely females, flashing away in the darkness. And recently, on the French border, Club Paradise opened with 180 sex workers, making it the biggest brothel in Europe.

The Spanish economy may be dangerously close to melt-down . . . but one area at least—prostitution—appears to be doing very nicely, thank you.

As the clubs get larger, the clients get younger. According to studies carried out for the Spanish Association for the Social Reintegration of Female Prostitutes (Apramp), back in 1998 the typical client was a 40-year-old married male. By 2005, however, the average age had dropped to 30—and it appears to be getting lower. "The kids are going because they see it as a quick way of getting what would take a lot longer to happen if they went to a disco," Alvaro says. "You've got the money, you choose the woman you want and it's all over and done with." His own logic is even more brutal: "I go when I don't have a girlfriend."

There is no single reason, though, why prostitution should be so popular in Spain. Historically it has long been seen as an expression of individual freedom—first as a pressure valve for the strait-laced family-focused environment of the Franco years [1939–75 under dictator Francisco Franco] (when prostitution was quietly ignored), and then consolidating itself after the dictator died. Then, as now, brothels would be listed in the yellow pages, albeit under the coy title of "nightclubs", and nobody batted an eyelid. Among the young men of the Spanish provinces, even in the late 1980s, sleeping with a prostitute was no longer something you did as a way of losing your virginity: it could actually be seen as cool.

In the 1990s, magazines such as *Interviú*, which prides itself on its investigative journalism, would think nothing of publishing "erotic guides to Spain". Even today, all-male business dinners can end up in the local "club". "Every now and then I have to take clients," says one accountant who did not want to be named, "but it's OK. They take credit cards."

If the roots of Spain's acceptance of prostitution ultimately lie with the sexual and personal repression of the Franco years, the most curious hangover from the sexual revolution is that, even today, most "serious" newspapers carry adverts for prostitutes. In the Madrid issue of one major national daily, 75 or 80 per cent of small ads are for prostitutes, offering all manner of services with prices from 20 to 200 [euros]. Plans to eliminate the so-called "contact ads" appear to be on a kind of permanent hold, partly justified by the precarious economic state of Spain's print media.

The Other Side of the Business

However, the underbelly of a trade which is legal in Spain but not recognised as an actual job is far from pleasant, with human trafficking constantly rearing its ugly head. In 2009 alone, Spain's Ministry of the Interior detected 17 international crime rings involved in sexual trafficking in Spain. Between January and April of this year [2010], according to the newspaper *El País*, the authorities identified 493 cases of women sold into sexual slavery.

Yet that makes no difference, it seems, to the clients who pour through the doors of the brothels. "There is a clear lack of awareness as to what is going on," says Marta González, a spokeswomen for the Madrid-based NGO [nongovernmental organisation] Proyecto Esperanza, which helps women who

Sexual Trafficking in Spain

Until recently, politicians adopted one of two stances on prostitution: it should be prohibited, or legalized. But a new phenomenon—immigration—has complicated the debate. According to statistics the government recognizes as accurate, 90 percent of sex workers are foreigners and 80 percent of the total are victims of trafficking. In other words, they did not choose to sell their bodies to make ends meet; these are women, controlled by mafias, who never had the luxury of choosing.

"Prostitution Without Slavery?
Human Trafficking Debate Divides Spain," El País.

have been victims of trafficking. "Clients don't realise that many of these women could be victims of trafficking. Lots of people would be more wary if the prostitutes were clearly under lock and key or had obviously been subject to physical abuse. They don't realise that all it takes is a death threat to their families back in Nigeria or Brazil, and the woman is already being coerced into prostitution."

The laws in Spain are of little help either, with prostitution currently a permitted activity—but with no labour rights. "They're already frequently leading a double life or are considered social outcasts and often are in dire need of money," said a Spanish Red Cross social worker running a health care programme for prostitutes. "Add the lack of legal rights, and they're a clear target for exploitation."

On top of that there's Spain's recession. "Economically the women I'm dealing with are at the end of their tether, and the lack of other employment possibilities makes everybody more nervous about keeping clients. In the process they put themselves at risk, too. They'll be more willing to accept it when a client doesn't want to use a condom, for example, to be sure they get him to sleep with them."

The underbelly of a trade which is legal in Spain but not recognised as an actual job is far from pleasant, with human trafficking constantly rearing its ugly head.

When prostitution and trafficking overlap, the legal situation grows even more discouraging. "Glitches in the legislation mean that an identical crime is punished less severely here than, say, in Germany," Ms Gonzalez says. "Forcing someone to prostitute themselves in Spain gets from two to four years in prison here, while human trafficking gets five to eight. But because the latter charge often can't be proved effectively because of poor legislation, the criminal gets the lower sentence."

Meanwhile, Spain's sex trade continues to flourish. And, in one way, it is literally more visible than ever: Recently, in an attempt to cut the number of road accidents, the police in Lerida, Catalunya, issued the prostitutes working in out-of-town lay-bys with fluorescent waistcoats.

Disaster Leaves Haitian Women in Danger of Being Human Trafficking Victims

Emilio Godoy

Emilio Godoy is a reporter for Inter Press Service (IPS) news agency. In the following viewpoint, he relays the warnings of experts and activists concerned about a rise in human trafficking in Haiti after the devastating 2010 earthquake, which left the country's government and law enforcement in shambles. Godoy reports that many of the women trafficked are smuggled through the Dominican Republic, which has failed to vigorously protect Haitian women and prosecute perpetrators.

As you read, consider the following questions:

1. How many people were killed in the January 2010 earthquake in Haiti, according to Godoy?

2. How many victims a year does the Mexican Ministry of Public Security claim fall prey to trafficking networks in Latin America?

3. How many Haitians a year were deported from the Dominican Republic between 2003 and 2008, according to the viewpoint?

Emilio Godoy, "Haitian Women at Increased Risk of Trafficking," Inter Press Service, September 24, 2010. Reproduced by permission.

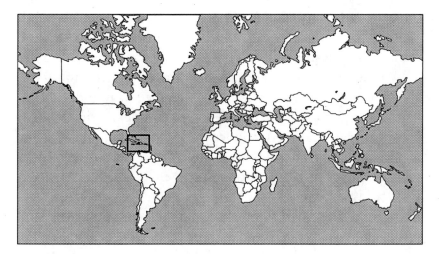

The January [2010] earthquake that devastated Haiti put women and girls in the poorest country in the hemisphere at an increased risk of falling prey to people trafficking, activists and experts warn.

"The phenomenon has become much more visible since the earthquake, with the increase in the forced displacement of persons," said Bridget Wooding, a researcher who specialises in immigration at the Latin American Faculty of Social Sciences (FLACSO) in the Dominican Republic, which shares the island of Hispaniola with Haiti.

The January [2010] earthquake that devastated Haiti put women and girls in the poorest country in the hemisphere at an increased risk of falling prey to people trafficking, activists and experts warn.

"There is huge vulnerability to a rise in human trafficking and smuggling," she told IPS [Inter Press Service].

The Dominican Republic and the United States are the main destinations for Haitian migrants. The figures vary, but there are between 500,000 and 800,000 Haitians and people of Haitian descent in the U.S. and between one and two million in the Dominican Republic.

Women in Haiti "are exposed to forced prostitution, rape, abandonment and pornography," Mesadieu Guylande, a Haitian expert with the Coalition Against Trafficking in Women-Latin America and the Caribbean (CATW-LAC), told IPS.

The situation in Haiti was one of the issues discussed by representatives of NGOs [nongovernmental organisations], experts and academics from throughout the region at the second Latin American conference on human smuggling and trafficking, which ran Tuesday through Friday [September 13–17, 2011] in Puebla, 130 km [kilometers] south of Mexico City.

What Is Human Trafficking?

The 7.0-magnitude quake that hit the Haitian capital on Jan. 12 and left a death toll of at least 220,000 forced tens of thousands of people to live in camps.

The United Nations [U.N.] defines human trafficking as "the recruitment, transportation, transfer, harbouring, or receipt of persons, by means of the threat or use of force or other forms of coercion, of abduction, of fraud, of deception, of the abuse of power or of a position of vulnerability or of the giving or receiving of payments or benefits to achieve the consent of a person having control over another person, for the purpose of exploitation."

Smuggling of persons, again according to the U.N., is limited to "the procurement of the illegal entry of a person into a state party of which the person is not a national or a permanent resident, in order to obtain, directly or indirectly, a financial or other material benefit."

The Scope of the Problem

In Latin America, an estimated 250,000 victims a year fall prey to trafficking networks, yielding a profit of 1.35 billion dollars for organized crime rings, according to statistics from the Mexican Ministry of Public Security. However, NGOs say the numbers could be higher.

Organisations like the CATW-LAC estimate that over five million girls and women have been trapped by these criminal networks in the region, and another 10 million are in danger of falling into their hands.

After the earthquake, the United Nations Stabilisation Mission in Haiti (MINUSTAH), which has been in the country since 2004, beefed up security along the porous border with the Dominican Republic.

Authorities in the Dominican Republic deported some 20,000 Haitians a year between 2003 and 2008, according to government figures.

Haitian Trafficking in the United States

Since the tragedy, the New York-based Sanctuary for Families, a nonprofit organisation dedicated to aiding victims of domestic violence and their children, has taken in some 100 Haitian women.

"They came illegally, with forged documents or with expired visas. We offer them shelter, financial assistance or legal advice," Dorchen Leidholdt, director of Sanctuary's Center for Battered Women's Legal Services, told IPS.

Thursday [September 23, 2010] was International Day Against the Sexual Exploitation and Trafficking of Women and Children, established in 1999 by the World Conference of the Coalition Against Trafficking in Women (CATW).

"We have evidence of a growth in trafficking and smuggling of persons, which is reflected in the increase in the number of children panhandling in the streets of Santo Domingo, for example," said Wooding, co-author of the 2004 book *Needed but Unwanted*, on Haitian immigration in the Dominican Republic.

The author was in Port-au-Prince when the quake hit.

Even before the disaster, some 500,000 children were not attending school in Haiti, a country of around 9.5 million people, Guylande said.

A Crime That Goes Unpunished

Since 2007, there have been no convictions in the Dominican Republic under Law 137-03 against trafficking and smuggling, passed in 2003, according to the U.S. State Department "Trafficking in Persons Report" 2009.

As a result, the State Department reported that the government of the Dominican Republic "does not fully comply with the minimum standards for the elimination of trafficking" and put the country on its Tier 2 Watch List.

In Haiti, things are no different. Although the government ratified the Protocol to Prevent, Suppress and Punish Trafficking in Persons, Especially Women and Children, supplementing the United Nations Convention Against Transnational Organized Crime, in force since Sept. 29, 2003, it has failed to implement its provisions in national laws.

"The penal system is fragile and the judiciary is neither independent nor trustworthy, a situation that works in favour of traffickers," Guylande said.

The only legal case brought in Haiti was against 10 U.S. missionaries who tried to take 33 children out of the country after the January catastrophe. However, they were acquitted of charges of smuggling children and released from prison.

Periodical and Internet Sources Bibliography

The following articles have been selected to supplement the diverse views presented in this chapter.

Haneen Dajani and Ola Salem | "Human Trafficking Cases Rising, Says Officials," *The National*, March 9, 2011.

Melissa Ditmore | "The Sweep of Modern-Day Slavery," *Guardian* (UK), June 25, 2009.

Deena Guzder | "International NGO Warns That the Global Recession Will Increase Human Trafficking," Pulitzer Center on Crisis Reporting, August 29, 2009. http://pultizercenter.org.

Paul Harris | "Forced Labour and Rape, the New Face of Slavery in America," *Observer* (UK), November 22, 2009.

IRIN | "Cambodia: Trafficking Domestic Workers to Malaysia," March 17, 2011. www.irinnews.org.

Siddharth Kara | "On the Trail of Human Trafficking: Forced Labor in Nepal," CNN, September 7, 2010. http://articles.cnn.com.

Elizabeth Lee | "Rights Activists Say China's Gender Ratio Contributes to Human Trafficking," VOAnews .com, January 24, 2011. www.voanews.com.

Sara Lerner | "Human Trafficking: Farm Labor, Forced Labor?" KUOW.org, March 18, 2010. www .kuow.org.

Abigail Pesta | "Diary of an Escaped Sex Slave," *Marie Claire*, October 9, 2009.

Fadli and Yuli Tri Suwarni | "Incidence of Human Trafficking High in Poverty-Stricken Areas," *Jakarta Post*, April 26, 2008.

GLOBALVIEWPOINTS

CHAPTER 3

Strategies to Reduce
Human Trafficking

UN Launches a Global Plan of Action to Combat Human Trafficking

United Nations Office on Drugs and Crime

The United Nations Office on Drugs and Crime (UNODC) is the agency tasked with fighting international crime and the illegal drug trade. In the following viewpoint, UNODC announces the United Nations Global Plan of Action to Combat Trafficking in Persons, a global strategy to bring governments together in order to coordinate effective policies to combat human trafficking. Under the plan, experts will emphasize gathering more data on human trafficking to better understand and fight the problem.

As you read, consider the following questions:

1. When was the United Nations Global Plan of Action to Combat Trafficking in Persons adopted by the UN General Assembly?

2. What kind of trust fund does the plan call for, according to the viewpoint?

3. According to UN estimates, how many people worldwide are being currently exploited as victims of human trafficking?

United Nations Office on Drugs and Crime, "United Nations Launches Global Plan of Action Against Human Trafficking," September 1, 2010. Reproduced by permission.

The United Nations Global Plan of Action to Combat Trafficking in Persons was adopted by the General Assembly on 30 July [2010] to urge Governments worldwide to take coordinated and consistent measures to try to defeat the scourge.

The Plan calls for integrating the fight against human trafficking into the United Nations' broader programmes to boost development and strengthen security around the world.

It also calls for the setting up of a United Nations voluntary trust fund for victims of trafficking, especially women and children.

A Clarion Call

Secretary-General Ban Ki-moon said that the Plan of Action should serve as "a clarion call" to Member States, international organizations and civil society groups of the need to take immediate steps "to stop this terrible crime against human dignity, which shames us all".

The United Nations has estimated that more than 2.4 million people are currently being exploited as victims of human trafficking.

"It is slavery in the modern age," Mr. Ban said. "Every year thousands of people, mainly women and children, are exploited by criminals who use them for forced labour or the sex trade. No country is immune. Almost all play a part, either as a source of trafficked people, transit point or destination."

The Key Is World Cooperation

The Secretary-General urged countries, philanthropists and others to contribute generously to the new trust fund for trafficking victims.

"The fund aims to help Governments, intergovernmental and nongovernmental organizations provide these vulnerable

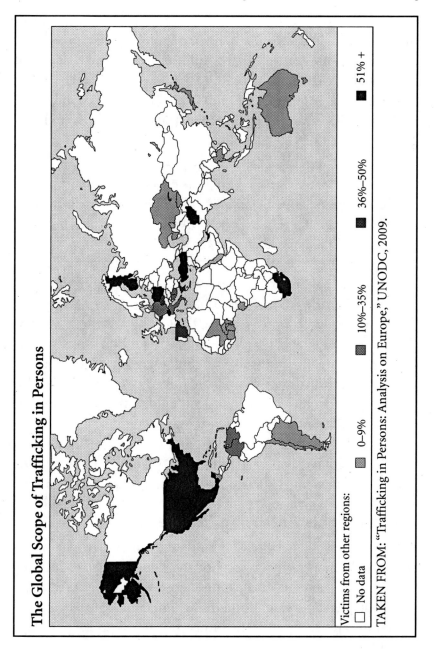

The Global Scope of Trafficking in Persons

Victims from other regions:

☐ No data ▨ 0–9% ▨ 10%–35% ▨ 36%–50% ■ 51% +

TAKEN FROM: "Trafficking in Persons: Analysis on Europe," UNODC, 2009.

people with protection and support for their physical, psychological and social recovery. After they have been exploited and abused, they should not be punished, too."

The Plan of Action—which focuses on preventing trafficking, prosecuting offenders and protecting victims—also stresses the importance of obtaining more research, data and analysis about the problem.

"We must improve our knowledge and understanding of this crime if we are to make good policy decisions and targeted interventions," Mr. Ban said.

The Plan of Action—which focuses on preventing trafficking, prosecuting offenders and protecting victims— also stresses the importance of obtaining more research, data and analysis about the problem.

"Within the United Nations system, my appreciation goes to UN.GIFT, the Vienna Forum, the Blue Heart Campaign and our goodwill ambassadors. UNODC's [United Nations Office on Drugs and Crime's] global report on human trafficking, anti-trafficking toolkits and manuals, documentary films, public information and technical assistance have also played a part to build consensus. I thank all those involved for their commitment and hard work," he said.

He added that the only way to end human trafficking is by working together, between States and within regions, among United Nations entities and in public-private partnerships.

Human Rights Are Being Violated

In his address, General Assembly President Ali Treki emphasized the human rights aspects of the fight against trafficking. "Abduction, coercion, trafficking across national and international borders, forcing women and children into sexual exploitation and servitude—this must not be accepted in today's world," he said.

"As this heinous crime flourishes, thousands of men, women and children are robbed of their safety, their freedom and their dignity. Human trafficking devastates families and tears communities apart. When the history of this horror calls, we cannot let this period be remembered as one in which the global community knew but did not act."

Canadian Leaders Urge Cooperation on a Global Plan to Fight Human Trafficking

Mark Kennedy

Mark Kennedy is a reporter for Postmedia News. In the following viewpoint, he examines the leadership role that Canadian prime minister Stephen Harper is taking on the issue of human trafficking, as evinced by his attempts to convince several government leaders at the 2010 Asia-Pacific Economic Cooperation forum to take action on the issue. Kennedy reports that Harper is actively working to bring the issue of human trafficking to the forefront and generate an urgency to devise a global plan to combat the practice.

As you read, consider the following questions:

1. How many political leaders attended the 2010 Asia-Pacific Economic Cooperation forum, according to the viewpoint?

2. In the author's view, what incident prompted Stephen Harper's declaration to crack down on human smuggling?

3. In late October 2010, how many Sri Lankans were arrested who were planning on being smuggled into Canada?

Mark Kennedy, "Harper Seeks International Help in Human Smuggling," Postmedia Network, November 13, 2010. Material Reprinted with the express permission of: "Postmedia News," a division of Postmedia Network, Inc.

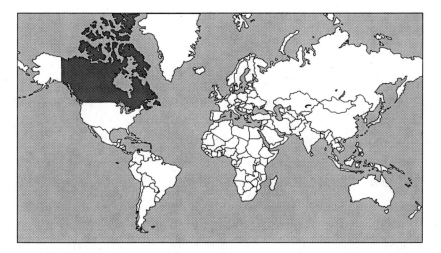

[Canadian] Prime Minister Stephen Harper urged leaders from other nations on Saturday [November 13, 2010] to help devise a global solution to the problem of human smuggling.

Mr. Harper lobbied for the comprehensive plan at the annual Asia-Pacific Economic Cooperation (APEC) forum.

The weekend gathering of 21 political leaders—mainly consisting of Asian countries, but also Canada, the U.S. and Mexico—is focusing this year on issues ranging from boosting trade to preventing terrorism.

Making Human Trafficking a Key Priority

But on the eve of the conference, as Harper was wrapping up the G-20 [a group of twenty financial leaders from around the world] summit in Seoul [South Korea], he publicly signaled his intention to also have "important talks" with his political counterparts about human smuggling.

Aides said that during a series of bilateral meetings Saturday, Harper raised the issue with APEC leaders from Malaysia, Philippines, Brunei, and Vietnam.

It's a reflection of his government's political plan to cast the spotlight—within Canada and internationally—on the problem.

The Harper government declared it would crack down on human smuggling after a ship carrying 492 refugees crossed the Pacific Ocean on a dilapidated ship called the *Sun Sea* to land in August on the shores of British Columbia.

The Tories have introduced legislation in Parliament which includes stiff penalties for smugglers and shipping companies that smuggle asylum-seekers into Canada.

There are also measures that penalize refugee claimants arriving in groups if they are deemed by the public safety minister to have paid smugglers to get them to Canada. Such asylum-seekers could be detained up to a year under the proposed bill.

Canada to Address Problem of Human Trafficking

But Mr. Harper said tighter domestic controls are only part of the solution to stopping "queue jumping and human smuggling."

"We are going to need stronger and more effective laws in Canada if we are going to deal with that problem."

"But we are also going to need—and we do have—greater cooperation internationally, particularly in the Asia-Pacific region, where a large portion of this problem begins."

The Conservative government has appointed a "special emissary," Ward Elcock, who has been holding meetings in recent weeks with officials in Asian countries. Harper said he will talk with political leaders about the progress of those intergovernmental discussions.

"The fact of the matter is, as you know, many countries who are much closer to the problem have much more severe difficulties than Canada does. But we obviously want to make sure we're part of a global solution, a regional solution, and that we don't allow further spillover of this problem into our country."

Australia's Struggle with the Problem

Political observers say finding a solution isn't as easy as Harper might think. In recent years, Australia has been the preferred destination for human smuggling rings and that country's government has tried to crack down—often to no avail.

Mark Riley, political editor for Australia's Seven Network, said human smuggling has been a "massive issue" in his country.

"There's a degree of xenophobia in the community, people who are scared about people from other countries coming in and taking that which is theirs. I think it's a shared concern in a lot of countries. I'm sure it's the same in Canada."

In recent years, Australia has been the preferred destination for human smuggling rings and that country's government has tried to crack down—often to no avail.

Mr. Riley said Australia has tried various techniques to disrupt the chain of human smuggling, but the asylum-seekers keep coming.

"The problem really is that you knock one of these snakehead organizations over and another three pop up."

Ultimately, said Mr. Riley, some are concluding the only solution is to stop the refugees from leaving their homelands.

"And you stop people leaving their own countries by giving them a quality of life, by giving them freedoms that they should enjoy in their own borders and governments that aren't corrupt and which respect the rights and privileges of their own people."

What Is Human Smuggling?

Human smuggling is a form of illegal migration involving the organized transport of a person across an international border, usually in exchange for a sum of money and sometimes in dangerous conditions. When the final destination is reached the business relationship ends, and the smuggler and the individual part company. In some cases, a person who has agreed to be smuggled into a country becomes a trafficking victim at the hands of the smuggler.

Royal Canadian Mounted Police,
"Frequently Asked Questions on Human Trafficking," 2011.

An International Plan Is Needed

Still, in Canada, the Harper government has pointed to more incidents which it says highlight the importance of an international action plan to stop smuggling.

In Thailand, in late October [2010], officials arrested 114 Sri Lankans. Immigration Minister Jason Kenney, who is spearheading the Tory government's anti-smuggling bill, said the Sri Lankans had been "planning to be smuggled to Canada."

The latest arrests follow an earlier Thai roundup in October of 155 Sri Lankans, some of whom were said then to be awaiting passage to Canada.

APEC leaders began their conference Saturday with a working luncheon, followed by a meeting with a business advisory council.

Conference Goals

The leaders are looking for ways to further liberalize trade in the region through a possible free trade agreement, ensure economic growth in the wake of the recession, and introduce measures to protect "human security."

The conference organizers have a broad definition for human security, saying the aim is to "reduce the threat to business and trade" in the region. Japan, for instance, is focusing on counterterrorism, security of food supplies, combating infectious disease and emergency preparedness.

At the plenary session where they discussed trade, the leaders sat in an oval room in which they were surrounded by an artificial bamboo forest.

And in the middle of the room, organizers had built a fake lake—reminiscent of the fake lake Canadian officials built to promote the Canadian outdoors for international journalists cooped up in a media centre at last June's G8 [a group of eight major world economies] and G-20 summits.

The difference is that while the Canadian version actually did have a few inches of water, the Japanese lake really is fake. It is a digital surface complete with virtual fish and waves.

Many political leaders were awestruck. Mr. Harper, peered into the lake and stopped to have his photo taken at it.

Great Britain Looks to Prosecute Human Traffickers More Effectively

Robert Booth

Robert Booth is a news reporter for the Guardian. *In the following viewpoint, he examines the Crown Prosecution Service's new policy on prosecuting human trafficking that focuses on providing support and informed advice to victims to encourage them to testify against their traffickers. Booth observes that this new policy was in response to criticism against the prosecutors, claiming they failed to gather enough evidence to garner trafficking convictions.*

As you read, consider the following questions:

1. According to the viewpoint, how many people were prosecuted for sex trafficking in Great Britain in 2009?
2. How many people were prosecuted for labor trafficking in Great Britain in 2009?
3. Why does Booth assert human trafficking victims are often reluctant to come forward to law enforcement?

Prosecutors have responded to criticism they are securing too few convictions for human trafficking by making a plea to victims to come forward and testify against their traffickers.

Robert Booth, "Prosecutors Call for Human Trafficking Victims to Testify," *The Guardian*, July 29, 2010. Reprinted by permission.

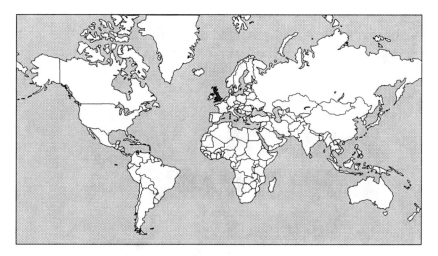

A New Plan of Attack

The director of public prosecutions, Keir Starmer, launched a draft policy on prosecuting a crime he described as "modern-day slavery" in a bid to increase the number of prosecutions for trafficking in England and Wales. Last year [2009] 102 people were prosecuted for sex trafficking and another 19 for labour trafficking.

The move comes as the Crown Prosecution Service [CPS] announced a growing problem of trafficking into Britain from Nigeria, Vietnam and China, which are believed to be the major source of victims, after many years in which eastern Europe had that status. In particular young women and girls are being trafficked from Nigeria to work as prostitutes, while boys and young men from Vietnam are being used in cannabis farms located in converted homes in residential areas across Britain. Victims of both sex are being trafficked from China into prostitution and forced labour such as domestic slavery, the CPS said.

"It is important that those who help victims understand our role in dealing with human trafficking cases," said Starmer. "This new public policy will be the go-to guide on the prosecution process for support groups ... and help them give in-

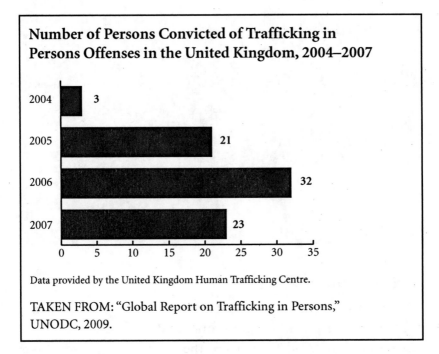

Number of Persons Convicted of Trafficking in Persons Offenses in the United Kingdom, 2004–2007

Data provided by the United Kingdom Human Trafficking Centre.

TAKEN FROM: "Global Report on Trafficking in Persons," UNODC, 2009.

formed advice to victims, which we hope will ultimately lead to more victims supporting prosecutions. Combating human trafficking is a high priority for the CPS and the criminal justice system—we are committed to tackling and disrupting this modern form of slavery."

Criticism of Past Prosecution Efforts

Campaigners for trafficking victims have been critical of the authorities' response to the crime.

"Over recent years the government has woefully underperformed in securing convictions for human trafficking," said Christine Beddoe, director of Ecpat UK. "There is no incentive for victims to come forward because of the lack of protection. Even recent efforts to improve the identification of victims through a national referral mechanism are being undermined by the Home Office's insistence on seeing too many of these exploited and vulnerable individuals as immigration offenders."

Victims are often reluctant to come forward because they fear retribution against themselves or their families back home and because they distrust the police, especially if they are from a country which suffers from a corrupt law enforcement system.

Campaigners for trafficking victims have been critical of the authorities' response to the crime.

The CPS wants victims to know they will be protected through the prosecution process and to encourage them to come forward with vital evidence against the person or gang that exploited them in order to secure a conviction.

The draft policy states that victims can be screened from the defendant in court, public galleries can be cleared and the victim can give evidence through a TV link, even from abroad if they have returned to their home country.

The Difficulty in Prosecuting Human Trafficking

Successful prosecutions have proved difficult in recent years, partly because prosecutors must present juries with evidence that the suspected trafficker recruited the victim and moved them, which often requires evidence from the home country; that the victim has been forced into exploitation; and of the exploitation itself. To show all these, the victim's own evidence is a key starting point for investigators.

The CPS wants charities and support groups who assist victims of trafficking to explain to them how the prosecution system in the UK will protect them if they come forward, and is calling on agencies such as the Health and Safety Executive, the department of work and pensions and the UK Border Agency which come across trafficking victims to do the same.

The Western Hemisphere Needs NGO Involvement to Confront Human Trafficking

Kelsey Cary

Kelsey Cary is a research assistant at the Council on Hemispheric Affairs. In the following viewpoint, she analyzes the findings of the 2010 "Trafficking in Persons Report" from the US State Department that argues that the United States and Latin American governments should more effectively coordinate attempts to provide assistance to nongovernmental organizations (NGOs) that offer aid and rehabilitation to trafficking victims. Cary recommends that this renewed and cooperative effort should focus on the scourge of child trafficking, especially the Haitian children known as restaveks.

As you read, consider the following questions:

1. What are the four grades mentioned by Cary that are included in the TIP report?

2. According to Cary, why is examining human trafficking in Mexico important to US-Mexican relations?

3. According to the TIP report, how many restaveks are there in Haiti?

Kelsey Cary, "Combating Human Trafficking in the Western Hemisphere: The Need for Increased NGO Involvement," *Guatemala Times*, July 29, 2010. Reproduced by permission.

Human trafficking is a global industry that transcends borders, regions, and cultures. Within the Western Hemisphere trafficking is an important issue that arguably helps to shape relations between Latin American and the United States. In June 2010, the State Department report on trafficking in persons (TIP) included, for the first time, in its ten year existence, a ranking allocated to the United States as well as 177 other countries.

The TIP report helps substantiate the claim that the United States and Latin American governments must strive to improve the lives of millions of innocent people who increasingly are victims of human trafficking. The restaveks [or restavecs], Haitian youth forced into domestic labor without compensation, exemplify the lack of protective measures against child trafficking who usually turn out to be the chief victims of trafficking.

The plight of these children, in Haiti and elsewhere throughout the region, reflect both the obvious and more subtle weaknesses in efforts to reduce human trafficking in Latin America. The trafficking of children is an immensely serious problem that regional governments paired with nongovernmental organizations (NGOs) must address. Moreover, the United States must actively engage with both the governments of other countries as well as foreign NGOs to facilitate this improvement.

The trafficking of children is an immensely serious problem that regional governments paired with nongovernmental organizations (NGOs) must address.

Difficulties in Definition: The Palermo Protocol

Defining human trafficking is quite controversial. Although human trafficking is universally condemned by the international community, individual nations struggle to implement measures that meet the standards under the United Nations [UN] Protocol to Prevent, Suppress and Punish Trafficking in Persons Especially Women and Children, more commonly known as the Palermo Protocol. It defines trafficking in persons as:

> the recruitment, transportation, transfer, harboring or re-ceipt of persons, by means of the threat or use of force to other forms of coercion of abduction, of fraud, of decep-tion, of the abuse of power of a position of vulnerability or of the giving or receiving of payments or benefits to achieve consent of a person having control over another person for the purpose of exploitation. Exploitation shall include, at a minimum, the exploitation of the prostitution of others or other forms of sexual exploitation, forced labor or services, slavery or practices similar to slavery, servitude or the re-moval of organs. . . . The consent of a victim of trafficking in persons to the intended exploitation set forth [above] shall be irrelevant where any of the means set forth [above] have been used.

Though the above definition discusses the illegality of both sex trafficking and labor trafficking, two significant weak-nesses remain. An article published by *Human Rights Quar-terly* stipulates that the Palermo Protocol fails to acknowledge the trafficking of persons within borders, and instead may fo-cus too heavily on the transfer of persons from one state to another. However, domestic trafficking exists in many Latin American countries, such as Haiti and Brazil. A second con-cern regarding the Protocol's definition is its inclusion in UN Convention [Against] Transnational Organized Crime. Its placement there seems fitting, as much of human trafficking comes as a consequence of the actions of organized crime groups; however, individual actors and small groups also are responsible for a significant portion of trafficking.

Human Trafficking Defined by the United States

Even though the UN instituted the Palermo Protocol, many Latin American countries use the United States' definition of human trafficking. The Victims of Trafficking and Violence Protection Act of 2000 (TVPA) defines trafficking as:

> sex trafficking in which a commercial sex act is induced by force, fraud, or coercion, or in which the person induced to perform such act has not attained 18 years of age; or . . . the recruitment, harboring, transportation, provision, or obtaining of a person for labor or services through the use of force, fraud, or coercion for the purpose of subjection to involuntary servitude, peonage, debt bondage, or slavery.

The U.S. government allots foreign aid in part based on the grade a country receives in the "Trafficking in Persons Report," thus explaining many regional governments' attempts to adhere to the U.S. definition rather than the one given by the United Nations.

The TIP Report

The U.S. State Department releases the TIP report annually. It discusses each country elaborating on improvements or regression and gives countries a grade: Tier 1, Tier 2, Tier 2-Watch or Tier 3. Tier 1 countries are those deemed to comply fully with the minimum requirements provided by the Victims of Trafficking and Violence Protection Act (TPVA). Tier 2 consists of nations that do not fully comply with the TPVA, but are making substantial attempts to do so, while Tier 2-Watch nations make these efforts as well, but still have a significant increase in the absolute number of trafficking victims. Tier 3 countries, such as the Dominican Republic, do not fulfill the minimum standards nor are they making attempts to do so. Some critics of the TIP report argue that some countries in the region attempt to meet TIP requirements out of fear of receiving a low rank in the compilation's annual report and therefore do not implement measures specific to the nature and dimensions of the tempo of trafficking that is occurring within a given country.

Others speculate that the status of diplomatic relations between the U.S. and Latin America serves as the driving force behind the grade each country receives. Opponents of the U.S., like Venezuela, unquestionably receive a lower grade, than a country like Colombia which is rewarded for supporting U.S. interests in the region. For example, the United States ranks Cuba (a country with which the U.S. lacks basic diplomatic relations) as a Tier 3 country while Colombia receives the rank of Tier 1. Moreover, in 2005, Latin America had a higher percentage of Tier 3 countries than any other region in the world.

Even though it is difficult to produce a completely unbiased account of government efforts against trafficking without being swayed by foreign policy objectives, the TIP could at least try to find a balance between ethical concern and broader U.S. geopolitical goals and interests. This equilibrium is particularly important with regards to Latin American countries because the concept of migration and human trafficking are closely related to one another. Illegal immigrants who travel up through Mexico and Central America lack legal protection and are therefore more vulnerable to becoming victims of human trafficking. Moreover, strict immigration policies, such as those in the United States, provide only limited opportunities for legal migration that would go to protect immigrants. Restrictive human trafficking measures implemented by other countries in the region are likely to reduce the amount of trafficking in the United States.

The TIP Report as a Tool

In an interview with COHA [Council on Hemispheric Affairs], Mark Lagon, former ambassador to combat trafficking

What Are Restavecs?

According to the [Jean R. Cadet Restavek Organization], restavec [or restavek] children are usually responsible for preparing the household meals, fetching water from the local well, cleaning inside and outside the house, doing laundry and emptying bedpans. They usually sleep on the floor separate from members of the family they serve, and are up at dawn before anyone else to do household work. Sometimes they're physically and sexually abused.

Elizabeth Cohen,
"Painful Plight of Haiti's 'Restavec' Children,"
CNN.com, January 29, 2010.

in persons and current senior advisor of corporate responsibility for LexisNexis, uses the case of Venezuela to refute some criticism of the TIP report: "I advocated for raising Venezuela to a better ranking. The integrity of the report requires acknowledging improvement because all in all, there is no reason to give countries anything but an objective assessment." In this capacity, Lagon contributed to global anti-trafficking policy and directed the compilation of the TIP report. Venezuela, a nation with which the United States has strained ties, had a Tier 3 rank in 2007, but in 2008, it was moved down a level to Tier 2-Watch class. Lagon views the TIP report as a constructive tool for improving relations between the U.S. and Latin America.

He describes the improvement in U.S.-Mexico relations with regards to human trafficking as a "quiet success," which in part is due to the State Department's decision to assign the U.S. a grade for the first time. Furthermore, Lagon contends, "Mexico continually hated any report where it was given a grade, but by including the U.S. in the TIP report we admitted, weaknesses in a way that we had not done before. Consequently, this dialogue has led to a more constructive relationship, fostering cooperation in regards to preventing human trafficking."

He went on to clarify that "the heart of human trafficking lies in exploitation; it's not always about migration. Forty percent of trafficking victims in the U.S. come from Latin America. It is every bit as much for labor as for sexual exploitation." A Congressional Research [Service] report highlights the case of Mexico because it accounted for twenty-three percent of recognized human trafficking victims in the U.S. in 2008 alone. Thus, increased collaboration between the U.S. and Mexico regarding immigration and trafficking legislation will only yield positive outcomes. By examining the case of Mexico it is evident that a deepening of relations between the U.S. and Latin American countries could be facilitated by engaging in dialogue regarding human rights, especially trafficking.

One of the most unsettling aspects of human trafficking is the exploitation of children used for sex tourism.

The Nature of Child Trafficking

Countries that do not provide programs to combat child trafficking often receive more condemnation and higher rankings in the TIP report. One of the most unsettling aspects of human trafficking is the exploitation of children used for sex tourism. A significant discrepancy exists in the legal age of consent for females in Latin American countries. Averages range from fourteen to eighteen years, the legal age as provided by the Palermo Protocol. These disparities make victim identification more difficult. A 2008 article published in *Human Rights Quarterly* reports that "other forms of trafficking include using children as panhandlers, news agents, garbage recyclers (i.e., those who sort through the public dumps for recyclable materials), domestic help, mining, agriculture, illegal adoption and child soldiers." These types of forced labor jobs frequently occur within the borders of one country, as with the restaveks in Haiti and child soldiers in Colombia.

A Focus on the Restaveks

The term restavek comes from a French word meaning "to stay" and refers to Haitian children who are forced into domestic labor without pay or guarantee of decent living conditions. According to the TIP report, there are 230,000 restaveks in Haiti who epitomize the concept that trafficking is not based solely on sexual exploitation. The United Nations Human Rights Council estimates that there are between 150,000 and 500,000 restaveks. Either figure still leads to the same conclusion: This form of exploitation should be of real concern to the island nation. Haitian society has historically been characterized by class stratification whereby authoritarian and hierarchal factors largely influence standards of living. In the most impoverished country in the hemisphere, adults regularly view children as economic commodities, which make them highly vulnerable to the perils of trafficking. Death of parents, runaways, and local sources of demand for child labor in urban centers and free trade zones are all factors that leave Haitian children open to exploitation.

Haiti has a long history of economic destitution. Seventy percent of the Port-au-Prince population was living in abject poverty even before the January 12th [2010] earthquake. Mark Lagon explains that this distress perpetuates human trafficking in that "the rule of law is lacking in Haiti and economic desperation only exacerbates the already dire status quo. Poverty is the driving force here. It leaves people vulnerable and it's likely to take decades if efforts are limited to fighting trafficking." Consequently, parents, if possible, will send their own children to stay with other families in urban areas based on the reasoning that these new caretakers will provide a better life than they themselves could. Unfortunately, this is not the case, as most end up subjected to little better than indentured servitude and then may have to work for their "owners" from birth to adulthood. Often these children must work from the early hours in the morning until the last household adult goes to bed. When discussing trafficking in Haiti specifically, Mark Lagon commented, "Restaveks suffer the most acute form of domestic servitude. In Haiti there's a permanent underclass locked in homes, paid little or nothing."

In order to improve the lives of Haitian restaveks as well as those of trafficking victims in general, a moral imperative must be present as well as the maintenance of a political system where everyone has equal access to justice, not just the wealthy elites. Additionally, trafficking usually occurs as a consequence of corruption that pervades all levels of society, from law enforcement to the judiciary. The United States has the capacity to assist other countries in the region to make laws become reality by helping train enforcement agencies, pressuring governments, to conduct themselves with rectitude and cooperating with NGOs that have proven themselves worthy of respect.

The UN Perspective on the Restaveks

Gulnara Shahinian, special rapporteur on contemporary forms of slavery, also articulated the manipulative nature of the restavek system in a BBC article in June 2009. She contends that it is equivalent to slavery through the ways in which it "deprives children of their family environment and violates their most basic rights such as rights to education, health, and food as well as subjecting them to multiple forms of abuse including economic exploitation, sexual violence, and corporal punishment, violating their fundamental right to protection from all forms of violence." This 'modern form of slavery' has proven difficult to suppress for a number of reasons. First, a law exists in Haiti stating that employers must pay people for their services, starting at the age of fifteen. This almost guarantees restaveks being thrown on to the streets at that age, adding to the chronic cycle of poverty in the country. Although Haiti is a signatory to the UN Convention on the Rights of the Child, it has no laws to protect restavek children and the likelihood of any law's effectiveness today would be limited. The January 12th earthquake has only made the situation worse, as both the Haitian National Police and NGOs have reported an increase in alleged cases of forced labor and forced prostitution of children and adults since the disaster. Haiti's inability to protect the most vulnerable societal demographic—children—reflects a problem rampant throughout the region and the world.

Human trafficking is a wealth-generating industry in which the risk to reward ratio eventually perpetuates the problem.

The Importance of NGOs

Increased cooperation between the U.S. and Latin American countries regarding laws as well as punitive measures will be crucial to countering the efforts of traffickers in the region, but the legal canvas is not necessarily the only area of concern. Lagon pointed to the problem of corruption among law enforcement officials who "tend to blame victims instead of help them." In order to assist victims not only in Haiti but also those to be found within the region, it is crucial that Washington [DC] step up its assistance to NGOs. For example, Polaris Project is an NGO that focuses on victim identification and then provides social services and transitional housing as called for by advocates of stronger federal anti-trafficking legislation. Another NGO, International Justice Mission (IJM), works in many locations, such as Guatemala, Peru, and Honduras, to rescue victims of human trafficking, particularly children, and bring justice to their perpetrators. Lagon explains that "we need to move the needle by extending the capacities of NGOs. They are often seen as an irritant, but are an essential part of civil society. By assisting NGOs financially, we can help build the capacity to decrease human trafficking." It is not merely a coincidence that Colombia which has a flawed human rights reputation, nevertheless received a Tier 1 ranking and is the largest recipient of U.S. aid in the region as well as being among Washington's primary military allies in the Caribbean.

Working Toward a Brighter Future

Human trafficking is a wealth-generating industry in which the risk to reward ratio eventually perpetuates the problem. A person can be exploited repeatedly, whereas drugs bear a one-time use restriction. This makes trafficking a lucrative matter for those involved. Tensions over definition and desensitization on the trafficking issue have only weakened efforts to prevent it. Consequently, the United States and governments in the region need to work together and thrust human trafficking into more of a spotlight. This must be done not merely once a year when the State Department releases the TIP report. Progress in the fight against human trafficking in the region will not come to fruition until the United States is willing to not only assist the governments of the Latin American countries, but also help NGOs identify as well as liberate victims. Washington must also resist any temptation to politicize the matter, as has been seen in the evaluation of Venezuela.

Sweden's Success in Fighting Human Trafficking Could Be a Model for Other Countries

Jonathan Power

Jonathan Power is a journalist. In the following viewpoint, he contends that Sweden's aggressive policy of prosecuting men who purchase sex has functioned to reduce cases of prostitution. Power notes that another benefit of Sweden's innovative law is that it has also reduced the practice of sex trafficking; as a result, Sweden has fewer incidents of child trafficking than other Scandinavian countries.

As you read, consider the following questions:

1. What percentage of human trafficking is related to sexual exploitation, according to the UN Office on Drugs and Crime?
2. When did Sweden pass its controversial law on prostitution?
3. How many Swedish males have paid for sexual services in their lives, according to estimates?

Helene Karle, the secretary-general of the Swedish branch of Ecpat [International], a worldwide organization based in Bangkok to counter the commercial sexual exploitation of

Jonathan Power, "Sweden's Success in Curbing Sex Trafficking," *Arab News*, November 3, 2010. Reproduced with permission.

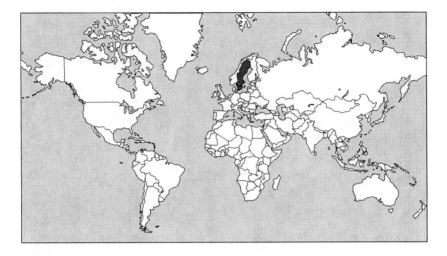

children, told me of two horrific incidents. The first was of a brothel in Thailand which caught fire. They found the bodies of 12–15-year-old girls tied to the beds. A second was of an 11-year-old girl killed by a man with a vibrator that broke inside her private parts. Neighbors, hearing her cries in the dark, rushed her to hospital but it was too late. She had lost too much blood.

The Problem of Sex Trafficking

Both of these incidents were girls "serving" foreign tourists. According to the UN [United Nations] Office on Drugs and Crime, "Several million people are the victims of human trafficking every year. About 80 percent is related to trafficking for sexual purposes. This trafficking is the third most profitable illegal activity after drugs and arms. In Europe alone 500,000 young women and girls are trafficked (usually from the East to Europe). Overall there are 2 million child victims a year and 1.2 million of these are trafficked—that's 2,700 a day". The rest are usually to be found in holiday places where they are abused by foreign pedophiles and others who can't resist the opportunity they are confronted with. In Europe, the EU [European Union] estimated in 2003 the problem of child porn had increased by 1,500 percent in the previous ten years.

What was a rather small problem escalated from the time of the Vietnam War, argues Karle, when resting American troops relaxed in Thailand and the Philippines. Heavy drinking and sex were the most common indulgence. Some also got involved in the porno film industry, often featuring children. Then they sold the films back home.

"The UN Convention on the Rights of the Child is the basis of our activity," she told me. "All the countries in the world have ratified it, apart from the US and Somalia."

Besides dealing with the issue at the receiving end, Swedish law enforcement cooperates with local authorities in Thailand, the Philippines and Eastern Europe. But the most important work has to be done at home, where the young girls work alongside older women who were often trafficked children when they started here.

When the law was introduced it was controversial. It criminalizes an age-old right to look at women's bodies as if they were goods to be bought or sold.

A Controversial Law

Since 1999 Sweden has had a law that hits at the demand side. It prohibits the purchase of services. Without demand there would be much less supply. Prostitutes are not punished, only the men. The reason for that law, as Detective Inspector [Jonas] Trolle, head of the [Human] Trafficking Commission of the Stockholm police, explains it, is "because prostitutes are the vulnerable ones in any sexual transaction."

The penalties for convicted men are not that severe. More important is the shame, when their families, friends and work colleagues learn of the transgression. They are paying a high

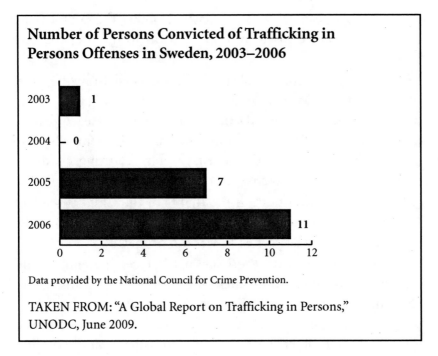

Number of Persons Convicted of Trafficking in Persons Offenses in Sweden, 2003–2006

Data provided by the National Council for Crime Prevention.

TAKEN FROM: "A Global Report on Trafficking in Persons," UNODC, June 2009.

price for their sexual appetite. This is the first law of its kind. Norway and Iceland have since emulated it.

Trolle estimates that one out of 14 Swedish males have bought sex at least once in their lives. The men come from all classes, all age groups and married or not. "Some are addicted to sex. Some do it because they seek power over a woman." Every other buyer of sex is married or in a relationship, and some 40 percent have children.

When the law was introduced it was controversial. It criminalizes an age-old right to look at women's bodies as if they were goods to be bought or sold. Even many women went along with the old practice—perhaps blithely assuming it is not their man who would ever look for a prostitute.

The Case of Holland

To measure Sweden's success one should compare it with the easy-going attitude of the government in Holland (although this is beginning to change with some brothels and sex shops being closed down). Holland has 20,000 prostitutes and there is no penalty for prostitution. The Dutch have long argued that it is best to keep it over ground than underground.

The Swedish legislation does work. Cases of street prostitution have fallen by more than half, although trafficking on the Net has increased the numbers again.

Before Sweden's ban, street prostitution and the trafficking of minors was about the same in all three Scandinavian countries. But after Sweden introduced its law Norway and Denmark found they had three times as many prostitutes as Sweden.

Not penalizing the young women or the teenage girls but punishing the men in a very visible way brings some significant success. Why don't other countries come and take a look at how they do it in Sweden?

Kenya Passes New Laws to Combat Human Trafficking More Effectively

IRIN

IRIN is an international news agency. In the following viewpoint, the reporter scrutinizes a new Kenyan law that legally defines and recognizes human trafficking as a crime. Previously, trafficking crimes fell under a variety of legal statutes, but law enforcement officials believe that the new law will be a valuable and effective tool in the fight against human trafficking.

As you read, consider the following questions:

1. Under the new Kenyan law, what is the penalty for those convicted of human trafficking?
2. According to the nongovernmental organization CRADLE, how many minors frequent "sex spots" at the Kenyan coast?
3. According to the author, why are there not any exact figures on the number of trafficking cases in Kenya?

Counter-trafficking specialists say a law recently passed in Kenya which, for the first time, legally defines and recognizes trafficking in persons as a crime, will help protect the vulnerable and assist survivors, while serving as a deterrent to perpetrators.

IRIN, "Kenya: Experts Welcome Counter-Trafficking Law," IRIN Africa, December 8, 2010. Reproduced by permission.

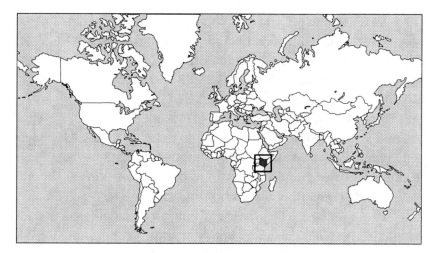

"This legislation represents a significant new tool for Kenya in counter-trafficking law enforcement," Tal Raviv, from the International Organization for Migration (IOM), said in a statement.

Raviv added: "We hope that the new Counter-Trafficking in Persons Act 2010 will create momentum to expand counter-trafficking initiatives in accordance with the 2008–2013 National Plan of Action."

Kenyan President Mwai Kibaki signed into law the new legislation in October [2010]. Conviction carries a 30-year jail term or a KSh30 million (US$370,000) fine.

Counter-trafficking specialists say a law recently passed in Kenya which ... legally defines and recognizes trafficking in persons as a crime, will help protect the vulnerable and assist survivors, while serving as a deterrent to perpetrators.

Necessary Legislation

In the past, absence of legislation and resources has affected law enforcement, officials said.

Claris Ogangah Onyango, the deputy executive director of the [International] Federation of Women Lawyers, told IRIN: "It will now be possible to institute proper charges, sustain successful cases and obtain deterrent sentences [for] all those involved in the practice."

Tony Odera, a lawyer at CRADLE, an NGO [nongovernmental organization] that works on children's issues through legal representation, said many cases of trafficking had been reported in the past but lack of a clear definition of the act had made prosecuting suspects complex.

"The new law will provide a comprehensive legal framework that would address issues pertaining to human trafficking," Odera said, adding that it will enable the establishment of a counter-trafficking in persons advisory committee and provide confidentiality during prosecution and compensation.

Previously, trafficking offences fell under a variety of legal statutes—the penal code, children's act and sexual offences act.

Sex Work and the New Law

Some poor parents and older persons are said to force children into prostitution. CRADLE estimates that about 1,500 minors frequent "sex spots" at the Kenyan coast.

According to Maurice Tsuma, the Coast Provincial Children's Officer, almost half the 150 children homes in Mombasa are not registered, raising concerns over their activities.

"We've raided some homes and closed them down but others come up; we are, however, keeping a close eye on them," Tsuma said.

In northern Kenya, frequent conflict and drought has made the region a fertile ground for those seeking cheap labour, young wives, even cattle raiders, say residents.

"Some women ferry young girls, offer them accommodation and food and recover the expenses by sending them on to the streets," Ahmed Set of the Islamic Foundation told

IRIN. "It is good that we [now] have a harsh way of punishing those people who ferry young children from remote parts of the region to work as herders [or] maids."

In Isiolo Town, in the north, IRIN spoke to Maria, 17, from the Ethiopian town of Moyale.

"I am Ethiopian but I attended primary school on the Kenyan side [of the border]," Maria said. "I completed Standard Eight two years ago [2008] but I did not continue with school. My friends told me education is not the only opportunity, they said my beauty, my body could help me earn a good living."

She told IRIN she had worked as a transactional sex worker to raise a KSh30,000 (US$375) trafficking fee to be paid to an agent, who would help her join friends working in some of Nairobi's massage parlours.

Dangerous Advertisements and Exploitation

According to a June [2010] trafficking in persons report by the US Department of State, Kenyans voluntarily migrate to the Middle East, other East African nations and Europe in search of employment, where they are exploited in domestic servitude, massage parlours and brothels, and forced manual labour, including in the construction industry. Chinese, Indian, and Pakistani women also reportedly go through Nairobi en route to work in Europe's sex trade.

Most of those trafficked are lured by bogus recruitment agents. Fake newspaper and Internet advertisements, false marriage proposals and deception by friends and relatives are used in internal trafficking for purposes of domestic or sex work, Alice Kimani, IOM's counter-trafficking project officer, told IRIN.

IOM has assisted the Kenya Association of Private Employment Agencies (KAPEA) in developing a recruitment code of conduct to prevent trafficking. Potential migrants are also encouraged to only use KAPEA or Ministry of Labour accredited agencies.

Kimani said more trafficking cases were being reported as awareness increased. However, she said, exact figures were not available.

"The lack of funding for research on the magnitude, the hidden and clandestine nature of this crime and the fact that it is only in recent years that people have begun to understand the issue has made it difficult to document the crime, in addition to the fact that there are still no reporting mechanisms that have been set up, and lastly not all victims seek assistance so there is no way of knowing how many are actually trafficked," Kimani said.

Australian Officials Need to Apply a Broader Vision to Address the Issue of Human Trafficking

Sharon Pickering and Marie Segrave

Sharon Pickering is an associate professor and Marie Segrave is a professor in the criminology department at Monash University; they are the authors of Sex Trafficking: International Context and Response. *In the following viewpoint, they consider the failure of a recent report by the Drugs and Crime Prevention Committee in Victoria, Australia, arguing that it misses the mark in dealing effectively with the crime of human trafficking because it relies too heavily on the problem of sex trafficking. Pickering and Segrave propose that the report should have examined all forms of human trafficking and presented a wider swath of recommended solutions.*

As you read, consider the following questions:

1. What do the authors believe the problem is with focusing exclusively on the sex industry?

2. How many trafficking-related offenses were investigated by federal police between 2004 and 2009?

3. How many trafficking-related offenses on average were investigated by federal police per month between 2004 and 2009?

Sharon Pickering and Marie Segrave, "Broader Vision Is Needed to Combat Human Trafficking," *Sydney Morning Herald*, June 21, 2010. Reproduced by permission.

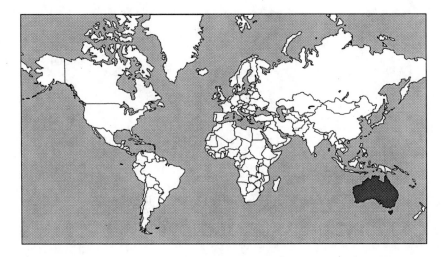

Human trafficking, particularly the trafficking of women into sexual servitude, is an issue that has captured the imagination of the community and policy makers in recent times—and late last year [2009] in Victoria, the Drugs and Crime Prevention Committee implemented an Inquiry into People Trafficking for Sex Work.

Internationally, efforts to address human trafficking have centred on extreme images and stories of women's sexual exploitation, eliciting emotive responses and measures that tend to focus on victim rescue and support, and punishment for offenders.

A Disappointing Effort

As researchers in this area, it is our challenge to question both the assumptions, the myths and the responses to this issue. Last year there was a chance for the Victorian community to move away from the reliance on rare cases of extreme exploitation, to consider the complexity of the issues and to draw on the findings from recent research. But the result was disappointing.

The report of the Inquiry into People Trafficking for Sex Work, tabled in the Victorian Parliament earlier this month

[June 2010], embodies the failure of the community to make the most of this opportunity. With 30 recommendations, the report seeks to develop a comprehensive state-based response to the trafficking of women for sexual purposes. But this significant suite of interventions was based on limited evidence. In fact, Judy Maddigan, chairwoman of the Drugs and Crime Prevention Committee, described it as "scanty" in the foreword.

As researchers in this area, it is our challenge to question both the assumptions, the myths and the responses to this issue.

We have a number of concerns. First, the inquiry was limited because of its exclusive focus on sex trafficking. Human trafficking occurs in a range of industries and involves exploitative practices that may include sexual, physical, emotional and/or financial abuse. Research shows that women trafficked into the sex industry are not necessarily sexually exploited and that men and women trafficked into other industries do experience sexual exploitation.

The risk we run of such a selective inquiry is a limited understanding of the broader realities that contribute to and sustain exploitative practices.

Understanding the Broader Issues

In our research and in reports last year in *The Age*, it is clear that exploitation and trafficking of temporary migrant workers occurs in many industries—including the hospitality and agricultural sectors—in Melbourne and across regional Victoria.

Focusing exclusively on the sex industry means that we are not being challenged to fix migrant worker vulnerabilities or to pay heed to Victoria's responsibility to ensure effective workplace regulation and migrant worker protection.

Child Trafficking in Australia

According to UNICEF [the United Nations Children's Fund], reported forms of child trafficking in an international context are known to involve labour exploitation, sexual exploitation, forced marriage, criminal activities, adoption, armed conflict and begging. While there are significant reports and publications focusing on the issue of child prostitution in Australia and child trafficking within Asia to satisfy the child sex industry, there is only limited anecdotal evidence of trafficking of children in Australia. As such it is not possible to estimate the extent of child trafficking in Australia or make generalised statements about the patterns of this phenomenon.

"Child Trafficking in Australia,"
TC Beirne School of Law, the University of Queensland, 2010.

The second concern is that the recommendations focus on Victoria adopting a state-based response to sex trafficking. This will work independently of the Commonwealth, which already operates and funds research, policing and victim support measures. This seems a significant waste of Victorian money and resources.

Diverting Resources

The report further recommends that Victoria Police divert current sexual offences resources to sex trafficking investigations. On the numbers, this makes no sense.

Between 2004 and 2009, federal police investigated 270 trafficking-related offences, an average of 30 cases nationally a year, compared with Victoria Police recording 1543 rape offences in 2008–09 alone.

There is no evidence in the report to justify an urgent intervention along these lines. In fact, such action has the potential to simply complicate data and compromise outcomes, as multiple agencies are then involved in developing anti-trafficking approaches, investigations and recording methods across Australia.

If this inquiry could be rewound and we had the opportunity to be involved in its creation, we would ask for an approach that engaged closely with human trafficking, in all its forms, and for consideration at both state and national levels of how to end the shameful trafficking in men, women and children both within and beyond our borders.

Cambodia Protects Women from Traffickers by Banning Marriage to South Korean Men

Brian McCartan

Brian McCartan is a journalist. In the following viewpoint, he reports that international marriage brokers are under increasing scrutiny as they are suspected of being fronts for human trafficking rings after numerous complaints about the exploitation of Cambodian women by prospective South Korean husbands. McCartan chronicles the response of the Cambodian government to the charges that involves launching an awareness campaign and banning the practice pending a thorough investigation by the proper authorities.

As you read, consider the following questions:

1. How many foreign marriage licenses were granted in Cambodia in 2007, according to the author?
2. According to the viewpoint, how many foreign marriages were registered in Cambodia in January 2008?
3. Why are foreign brides so popular in South Korea, in the author's opinion?

Brian McCartan, "Not All Bliss for Take-Away Cambodian Brides," *Asia Times*, April 8, 2008. Reproduced with permission.

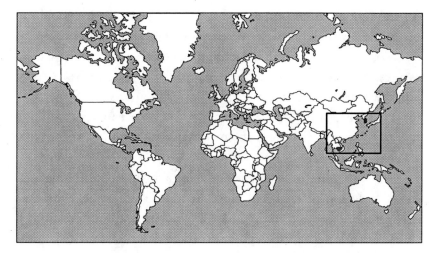

As Cambodia's once war-shattered, now booming economy opens to the world, Cambodian women are leaving in droves as several international marriage brokers have established matchmaking services in the impoverished country. Operating in a shadowy legal space, questions have been raised about the possible exploitative nature of the business, which some contend has acted as a front for global human trafficking rings.

Last week [March 30–April 5, 2008], the Cambodian government moved to put that trade on hold while it investigates whether any of the international brokers have ties to underworld crime syndicates. The Geneva-based International Organization for Migration (IOM) had earlier drawn attention to the trade and is scheduled to release next month an investigative report on the growing numbers of South Korean men who come to Cambodia in search of brides.

A Shady Practice

The mechanics of the trade are still murky. What is known is that women from mostly rural areas are brought by brokers into the capital city of Phnom Penh and put on display for prospective foreign grooms. The brokers are usually either informal operators or connected to one of several matchmaking businesses, which until now operated freely in Cambodia.

Most of the women who contract with the matchmaking services are in their teens or early 20s and usually from rural areas where they have received basic, if any, schooling. The IOM's report says "the vast majority of [Korean-Cambodian] marriages occur through an informal and exploitative broker-arranged process."

The introductions are more transactional than romantic. Bride selection often takes place in hotel restaurants where as many as 100 women, the IOM report claims, are lined up and put on display for prospective grooms. After a woman is chosen, details are worked out between the groom and bride-to-be and the broker.

A marriage is held after a few days, followed in some cases with a short honeymoon. The groom then returns to his home country while paperwork is processed for his new wife to follow. In 2007, the number of foreign marriage licenses rose to 1,759, up from a mere 72 in 2004. There were 160 foreign marriages registered in Cambodia in January of this year.

South Koreans make up a large percentage of the men seeking brides in Cambodia. In 2005, marriages to foreigners accounted for 14% of all marriages in South Korea, up from 4% in 2000. According to the United States 2007 "Trafficking in Persons Report," 72% of South Korean men in foreign marriages marry women from Southeast Asia or Mongolia. They are often lured by billboards which dot the South Korean countryside, advertising marriage services to foreigners.

Marriage Tours

Rural governments have even been known to subsidize marriage tours as a way of dealing with growing rural depopulation. The South Korean marriage brokering business began in the late 1990s, where it first aimed to pair Korean farmers or physically handicapped men with ethnic Koreans from China.

The Korean Consumer Protection Board claims 2,000 to 3,000 marriage agencies now operate in South Korea.

Marriage tours also began in Vietnam and by 2007 the number of South Korean marriages to Vietnamese women ranked second only to brides from China. The search for foreign brides has been driven by low birth rates and the growing difficulty South Korean men have finding brides among the country's newly ambitious young females.

Many of the men coming on marriage tours to Cambodia have already arranged contacts through online services, which usually host images of eligible women on their websites. One such service is "Mr Cupid," which offers Cambodian, Vietnamese, Vietnamese Muslim and Chinese women. The agency, which has been operating since 1993 from Singapore and does not cater specifically to South Koreans, claims to customers to "transform your life in six days!"

Its operations were expanded beyond Vietnam to Cambodia and China in 2000 and Mr Cupid's website also offers franchise services. The website claims, "Come to Cambodia today and we guarantee that your visit will be fruitful, you will find the lady of your dreams waiting for you right there." From services like this, or those based in South Korea, men can arrange four- to six-day marriage tours.

Match Made in Hell

In many ways such services are false advertising. Marriages between Cambodian women and South Korean men are known to be fraught with difficulties, frequently caused by huge cultural and linguistic divides. "Often the women have misguided expectations of what life may be like abroad; there is a lack of realistic information about life in Korea," the IOM's report says.

Indeed, most of the women's fantasies of what their new lives will be like are based on Korean movies and television shows that have recently gained popularity in Cambodia and

The Case for Marriage Brokers

The widespread availability of sex-screening technology for pregnant women since the 1980s has resulted in the birth of a disproportionate number of South Korean males. What is more, South Korea's growing wealth has increased women's educational and employment opportunities, even as it has led to rising divorce rates and plummeting birthrates.

"Nowadays, Korean women have higher standards," said Lee Eun-tae, the owner of Interwedding, an agency that last year [2006] matched 400 Korean bachelors with brides from Vietnam, China, the Philippines, Mongolia, Thailand, Cambodia, Uzbekistan and Indonesia. "If a man has only a high school degree, or lives with his mother, or works only at a small- or medium-size company, or is short or older, or lives in the countryside, he'll find it very difficult to marry in Korea."

Norimitsu Onishi,
"Korean Men Use Brokers to Find Brides in Vietnam,"
New York Times, February 22, 2007.

other parts of Asia. The new Cambodian brides often expect their South Korean grooms to be rich, successful businessmen; the reality, however, as the IOM report explains, is that they are often poor and poorly educated. This impacts the women's hopes that through marriage they would be able to send money home to support their families.

The pressures often result in disappointment and physical abuse. The deaths of several Vietnamese wives in South Korea in 2007 and early 2008 due to mistreatment by their South Korean husbands have already raised hard questions about the trade in Vietnam. One case that made headlines in both Vietnam and Cambodia involved the death of Tran Thanh Lan, a purchased bride who jumped or fell from her 14th floor balcony after only six weeks of marriage in South Korea. Her mother recently went to the country to demand an inquiry into her daughter's death.

Because the business apparently lacks a coercive element—women are allowed to turn down a marriage offer—it is not technically considered human trafficking. The business side of the trade, however, is certainly exploitative. Potential grooms pay as much as US$20,000 to brokers for their services, while the bride's family is given $1,000 as well as money to cover the costs of the wedding. The broker and agency divvy up the rest of the spoils.

Marriages between Cambodian women and South Korean men are known to be fraught with difficulties, frequently caused by huge cultural and linguistic divides.

Cases of Human Trafficking

The IOM report indicates that while there have been cases of abuse and domestic violence, "human trafficking has been far more difficult to identify." This may be the case in Cambodia so far, but there is plenty of documentation of Vietnamese women tricked by marriage brokers into factory work in South Korea. On February 26, police in Busan, South Korea, arrested a Vietnamese woman under suspicion of arranging sham marriages for $10,000 each. Once the purchased brides receive Korean citizenship, the women were divorced from their husbands and forced to work in factories.

Abuse against Cambodian brides has also been reported and some have ended up running away from bad marriages. The 2007 US "Trafficking in Persons Report" said, "NGOs [nongovernmental organizations] are reporting cases of foreign women placed in conditions of commercial sexual exploitation or forced labor by fake 'husbands' who work for trafficking rings or exploitative husbands who feel they 'own' the woman and can use her as a farm hand or domestic worker."

After recent crackdowns on the trade by Vietnamese authorities, the marriage brokering industry has grown rapidly in Cambodia, leading some trafficking experts to conclude that the brokers and trafficking rings have simply shifted countries. Marriage brokering is now illegal in Vietnam, but at its peak 20,000 brides were leaving the country every year.

Current Vietnamese law allows only the establishment of marriage support centers by nonprofit women's groups. The Vietnamese Ministry of Justice has recently recommended legalizing the service in order to place stricter controls on it. The police, however, have recommended raising penalties, making the offering of Vietnamese women as brides on a par with human trafficking.

The Cambodian government first publicly acknowledged a potential problem in March. Sar Kheng, deputy prime minister and minister of interior, said at the launch of a national anti-trafficking awareness campaign that some cases of human trafficking had been identified in the Cambodia marriage industry. Prime Minister Hun Sen has since ordered a crackdown on the industry, including cancellation of the licenses of two South Korean companies engaged in the trade.

Japanese Anti-Trafficking Activists Make a Difference

Thomasina Larkin

Thomasina Larkin is a writer for the Japan Times. *In the following viewpoint, she highlights the important work one group, Polaris Project, is doing to help foreign victims of sex trafficking in Japan, asserting that it has made noteworthy progress in bringing attention to the problem. Larkin also explores the organization's efforts in confronting the exploitation of Japanese women who are being victimized by a culture of inequality and sexual objectification; this has proven to be a difficult problem to address.*

As you read, consider the following questions:

1. According to the viewpoint, who is Shihoko Fujiwara?

2. How many volunteers did Fujiwara bring to Polaris Project from 2005 to the time this viewpoint was written?

3. Why does Fujiwara say it is difficult to make contact with Japanese victims of human trafficking?

"Neary grew up in rural Cambodia. Her parents died when she was a child, and in an effort to give her a better life, her sister married her off when she was 17. Three months later, they went to visit a fishing village. Her husband

Thomasina Larkin, "Putting the Red Light on Human Trafficking," *The Japan Times*, September 29, 2007. Reproduced by permission.

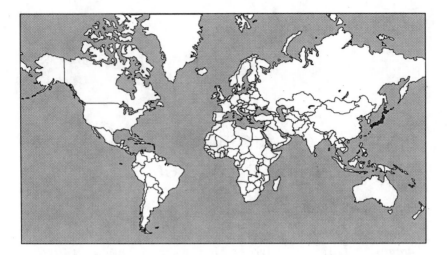

rented a room in what Neary thought was a guest house. But when she woke the next morning, her husband was gone.

"The owner of the house told her she had been sold by her husband for $300 and that she was actually in a brothel. For five years, Neary was raped by five to seven men every day. In addition to brutal physical abuse, Neary was infected with HIV and contracted AIDS.

"The brothel threw her out when she became sick, and she eventually found her way to a local shelter. She died of HIV/AIDS at the age of 23."

Neary's story, posted on Georgetown University's website, is just one of a portion of such stories that actually get reported each year.

Hundreds of thousands of other stories are never heard, and remain cloaked in the dark underworld of human trafficking—a world Shihoko Fujiwara first heard about while attending college in the U.S. in 2004.

A Submissive Culture

"I learned about the internal trafficking of Thai women to foreigners, to men from Germany or America or Japan," Fujiwara says, adding that the status of women in her home country then started to become more obvious to her. "That's when the issue became personal for me. Every time I came back to Japan, I felt so pressured. Society expects women to be feminine and submissive."

Fujiwara realized that this form of passivity was just a scratch on the surface of a much larger issue, one into which she felt compelled to dig deeper.

She searched the Internet for organizations in the U.S. that help combat the sex slave industry and she soon found Polaris Project, which just happened to be looking for Japanese-speaking volunteers to help launch a Tokyo branch.

HumanTrafficking.org reported in 2005 that an estimated 150,000 trafficking victims could be working in Japan, according to the Switzerland-based International Organization for Migration.

Getting Involved

Fujiwara's dedication was put to the test from the get-go.

"I worked all day at Polaris and during the night I worked at a restaurant," Fujiwara says. "I saw the development of the anti-trafficking movement in the U.S., and then after a year I was finally able to come back to Japan to launch Polaris here."

HumanTrafficking.org reported in 2005 that an estimated 150,000 trafficking victims could be working in Japan, according to the Switzerland-based International Organization for Migration.

It wasn't long before Fujiwara would find herself flooded with work.

Since 2005, Fujiwara has brought on 40 more volunteers and interns, started a multilingual outreach hotline, held seminars across the country, advocated for better anti-trafficking laws, organized workshops with police officers and embassies, run awareness-raising campaigns on college campuses and helped raise awareness among the victims themselves.

"When we met this one woman, she had called us three times before she finally trusted us and understood that she was being trafficked," Fujiwara says.

"Her brothel owner was forcing her to sleep with women and men and if she failed to do so she threatened her: 'If you don't go out with these people, I'll tell your family in your home country what you're doing here—selling your body—and your family will reject you,'" Fujiwara recalls of one of more than 340 cases Polaris Japan has heard. "She was psychologically controlled by her traffickers."

Domestic Exploitation in Japan

For the first couple of years, all of Polaris's clients in Japan were foreign women. But Fujiwara decided last year [2006] to start focusing on Japanese women.

"There's a lot of gender inequality here. It's a culture of seeing women as sex objects," Fujiwara says. "If you look at men's magazines, you always see naked women. Even women's and teen's magazines have strange info on how to be loved by your boyfriend, or how to please your man, which gives readers the wrong ideas about sex.

"I just want to have a healthy and safe environment for women and men," she says, adding that Polaris teaches about how condoms protect against STDs [sexually transmitted diseases] and that women should wait until they're ready to have sex. "All these things are so connected to adults, who are uncomfortable talking about sex and who learn about it from magazines, which are violent and objectify women. Men see those magazines and they go to sex parlors."

However, after two years of research, Fujiwara still finds it difficult to make contact with Japanese victims.

"The sex industry here is so much under the realm of entertainment," she says. "Women are being told that their job is fun, easy and that they can make money instantly for clothes and bags or debts. They're being glorified in media such as TV and magazines.

"I'm not against women's work," Fujiwara says. "I'm just so afraid the industry tries to hide the reality of the exploited women."

Fujiwara hopes a photo exhibition called "Human Trafficking—Unrecognized Reality" Oct. 12–13 [2007] at the Tokyo Women's Plaza forum in Shibuya, Tokyo, will help further shed some light onto the shady underworld of human trafficking.

Canada Launches an Anti-Trafficking Campaign

Joanna Smith

Joanna Smith is a reporter for the Toronto Star. *In the following viewpoint, she scrutinizes the Canadian campaign to raise awareness about the problem of human trafficking that involves pleas for Canadians to call in and report any suspicious activity to the proper authorities. Smith contends that some officials are skeptical about the campaign's efficacy, arguing that greater coordination of efforts among police, prosecutors, and social agencies is the key to addressing the crime.*

As you read, consider the following questions:

1. What do the "Blue Blindfold" campaign print, radio, and television spots look like, according to Smith?
2. How much did the Canadian government devote in the 2007 budget to combat human trafficking and child sexual exploitation?
3. How did the Conservatives vote on a 2009 Liberal motion calling for a plan of action to deal with human trafficking and sexual exploitation?

The federal government has launched an awareness campaign to urge Canadians to stop turning a blind eye to potential victims of human trafficking and anonymously report what they see.

Joanna Smith, "Feds Launch Human Trafficking Awareness Campaign," *Toronto Star*, September 7, 2010. Reproduced with permission.

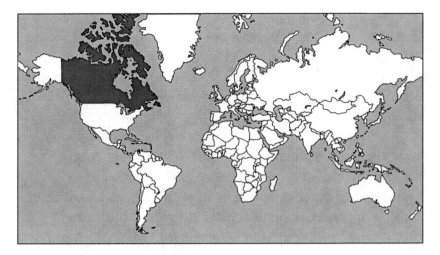

Public Safety Canada teamed up with the Canadian Crime Stoppers Association and the RCMP [Royal Canadian Mounted Police] for a public awareness campaign that aims to help the public—through what Public Safety Minister Vic Toews called "disturbing and uncomfortable" re-enactments of criminal exploitation—identify and report cases of human trafficking to authorities.

"It's going to help address one of the vilest crimes imaginable, that of human trafficking—a crime that is often referred to as modern-day slavery," Toews said in Winnipeg on Tuesday [in September 2010] as he announced the beginning of the "Blue Blindfold" campaign, which follows new mandatory minimum sentences for human traffickers that became law earlier this summer.

The "Blue Blindfold" Campaign

The print, radio and television spots will feature ordinary people with blue scarves tied around their eyes going about their daily lives as actors portraying victims engaged in forced labour such as serving drinks at a cocktail party and washing dishes.

"While we enjoy, we forget who's getting hurt," a voice-over in one of the television spots says as a woman wearing only lingerie and fishnet stockings dances around a pole, her male customers wearing blue blindfolds as they sit drinking around a table. "We see who we want and close our eyes to the rest."

The advertisements and educational brochures and posters urge the public to contact the Crime Stoppers anonymous toll-free hotline to report any suspicious activity.

"Some of the images you will see in this campaign are disturbing and uncomfortable. This is because this crime is disturbing and uncomfortable and it needs to be stopped," said Toews.

A More Comprehensive Approach

Critics and observers agreed that raising awareness is a good thing but questioned how much of a difference a tip line could really make without the proper resources to follow up on complaints and protect the victims once the crimes they are involved in come to light.

"We have been urging the government for a very long time to adopt changes to the law to make it clear that victims of trafficking should be treated as victims of a crime that need protection and not as people who should be detained and deported," said Janet Dench, executive director of the Canadian Council for Refugees.

> *Critics and observers agreed that raising awareness is a good thing but questioned how much of a difference a tip line could really make without the proper resources to follow up on complaints.*

Others called for a more comprehensive approach.

"Our law enforcement resources already come out overstrained and a new priority won't help much unless there are some resources to go with it," said John Thompson, an intelligence expert and president of the Toronto-based Mackenzie Institute.

"The tip line might be useful, but the long and short of it is you actually have to go after the smugglers and the traffickers and go after the people who use them ... (and) eliminate the customer base," Thompson said.

Allocating Resources Effectively

Chris McCluskey, a spokesman for Toews, said the government devoted $6 million in the 2007 budget to combat child sexual exploitation and trafficking, including law enforcement capacity, public education to increase the likelihood that these crimes will be reported and support for research.

Liberal MP [member of Parliament] Mark Holland (Ajax-Pickering), the public safety critic, said coordination of efforts among police, prosecutors and social agencies is the best way to fight human trafficking.

"I think that giving harsher sentences and campaigns that raise awareness won't take the place of those kinds of actions," said Holland, noting the Conservatives voted against a Liberal motion last year [2009] calling for a plan of action for dealing with human trafficking and sexual exploitation leading up to the 2010 Vancouver Winter Olympics.

"It's something that I think we all want to see curtailed and dealt with," said New Democrat MP and public safety critic Don Davies (Vancouver Kingsway). "I'm not sure that these measures are going to do a lot in that regard."

Address Smuggling and Trafficking

The awareness campaign comes at a time when the Conservative government is struggling with how to handle a boatload of Tamil refugee claimants from Sri Lanka, and Dench said she is concerned politicians are conflating the activities of human smuggling and trafficking in their response.

Toews acknowledged the distinction between the two activities, but also said that sometimes smuggling can turn into trafficking.

Toews told CBC TV that he and Immigration Minister Jason Kenney, who said in Paris on Monday that Parliament needs to consider mandatory minimum sentences for human smuggling, are in discussions on how to respond to the "twin and in many ways separate threats."

"I think we have to be responsive to new kinds of threats to our security, whether that's from the outside, or whether it impacts adversely on the personal integrity of people who are already here," Toews said, who signalled a change in law could be on the way. "I wouldn't be surprised to see something come forward in the next little while, whether it's a mix of law and policy or one or the other."

Periodical and Internet Sources Bibliography

The following articles have been selected to supplement the diverse views presented in this chapter.

Brendan Brady	"No Longer a Pedophile's Haven," *Newsweek*, November 16, 2010.
Billy Briggs	"Child Trafficking in Scotland Is Hidden Scandal, Says Report," *Guardian* (UK), March 13, 2011.
Tamara Cherry	"Human Trafficking Bill Passes Senate," *Toronto Sun*, June 17, 2010.
Gary Feuerberg	"Chinese Regime's Approach to Human Trafficking Critiqued," *Epoch Times*, August 24, 2010.
Rana Akbari Fitriawan	"Cultural Attitudes Blamed for High Human Trafficking Cases," *Jakarta Post*, February 5, 2010.
Martin Fletcher	"Call for Halt to Haiti Adoptions over Traffickers," *Times* (London), January 23, 2010.
Merle David Kellerhals Jr.	"United States and Ukraine Fight Human Trafficking," *Philadelphia News*, February 17, 2011.
Amanda Kloer	"Saudi Arabia Increases Trafficking Penalties," Change.org, July 15, 2009. http://news.change.org.
Ryan Messmore	"Fighting Human Trafficking Requires Multiple Institutions," *The Foundry* (blog), January 20, 2010. http://blog.heritage.org.
Xanthe Whittaker	"Trafficking Laws Are Anti-Immigration Laws," Joint Council for the Welfare of Immigrants, December 9, 2010. https://jcwi.wordpress.com.

CHAPTER 4

Aiding the Victims of
Human Trafficking

Ghana Struggles to Reintegrate Human Trafficking Victims into Society

Lucy Newman

Lucy Newman is a contributor to the Guardian. *In the following viewpoint, she chronicles the efforts of a nongovernmental organization in Ghana that is working to help the victims of human trafficking reintegrate into society. Newman reports that there is conflict between traditional Ghanaian counseling methods and Western ones, and experts say that Western methods must be adapted and fused with traditional methods in order to be accepted and practiced in certain contexts and regions of Ghana.*

As you read, consider the following questions:

1. According to estimates, how many victims of human trafficking were there in Ghana in 2008–2009?
2. For how much does Abdulai Danaah say impoverished parents sell their children in Ghana?
3. Why is there a distrust of Western counseling methods in traditional Ghanaian communities?

Ayi was fifteen when her parents sold her. She was sent to the Ghanaian capital of Accra, where her tasks included carrying heavy loads for market women. After a year she was

Lucy Newman, "Ghana Trafficking Victims Find Care and Comfort in Numbers," *The Guardian*, September 22, 2010. Reproduced by permission.

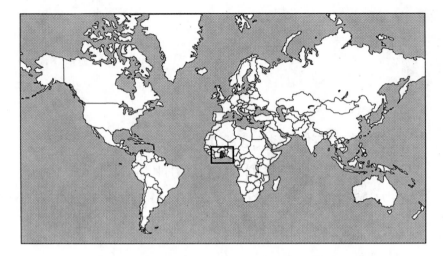

forced to work as a prostitute. "I was given drugs and received clients day and night," she says. Police were told of her plight by an NGO [nongovernmental organisation] and they arrested two men who were suspected of having trafficked her.

That NGO, the Centre for the Initiative Against Human Trafficking (CIAHT), helped Ayi back to her home town of Tamale, in the north of Ghana.

Ayi's story is far from unique, says Abdulai Danaah, CIAHT's national co-ordinator. Those trafficked can be subjected to sexual exploitation and forced labour. Although numbers are difficult to establish, Ghana's immigration services estimated in 2008–2009 there were some 12,000 victims of human trafficking.

Parents sell their children, sometimes for as little as $230, because of extreme poverty, Danaah says. They are often deceived into thinking their children will be treated well.

Tamale, where CIAHT is based, is the capital of northern Ghana. The region is the poorest in the country.

Rebuilding a Victim's Life

The challenge of rebuilding a life after being trafficked is great. Some of the women are ill and have sexually transmitted diseases. Research conducted in 2003 in nine countries by Melissa Farley, an American clinical psychologist and researcher, found high rates of violence, post-traumatic stress disorder and depression.

Many of these trafficked women have no formal skills and fall back into poverty. The psychological effects of their experiences can make it difficult to reintegrate into society.

That's where CIAHT comes in. The organisation teaches skills for employment to those who have been trafficked and provides groups with loans to help them get businesses up and running. It also gives medical and psychological assistance.

The challenge of rebuilding a life after being trafficked is great.

Ayi lived in a rescue house funded by CIAHT and received an hour of counselling, twice a week, for six months from a local priest.

"It is crucial not to reintegrate victims of trafficking back into society too quickly," Danaah says. "A key part of the counselling is to improve the self-image of the women so they feel they can be part of and contribute to their communities. It is also key that once the businesses are set up and running CIAHT continues long-term, low-level involvement to make sure that the ventures continue to be successful and the women feel supported."

The Role of Peer Counselling

Peer counselling also plays a part. One government official in Foushegu, a community outside Tamale, has been instrumental in getting such services in place, albeit on a small scale. "In the community of Foushegu the local church contacted me as it identified the need for counselling for victims of human trafficking," Prince Mohamed said.

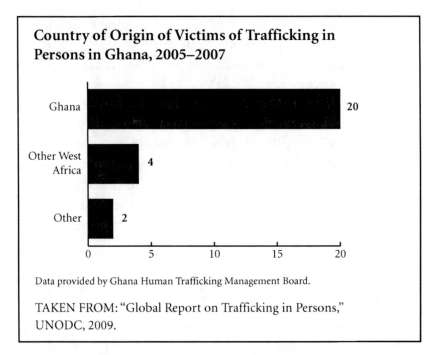

Country of Origin of Victims of Trafficking in Persons in Ghana, 2005–2007

Data provided by Ghana Human Trafficking Management Board.

TAKEN FROM: "Global Report on Trafficking in Persons," UNODC, 2009.

"We have set up peer counselling workshops to encourage people who have been trafficked to share their experiences and to support each other. The workshops also mean that the wider community is educated about the dangers of trafficking. The community really benefits from the discussions and have requested more sessions."

There's no clinical psychologist in Tamale to assist. Counselling services, when available, can be offered by local NGOs in collaboration with government and religious leaders, and they vary in quality and quantity. A lack of funding from Accra is the biggest constraint to greater care, and an issue that bedevils CIAHT.

Cultural Factors Influence the Reintegration Process

Other factors at play include controversy over what kind of counselling should be offered. The traditional Ghanaian definition of counselling can differ greatly from Western models.

In the West, mental health counselling is offered by someone in the discipline with a qualification. This simply isn't applicable in most African countries, including Ghana, where trained professionals are lacking.

In traditional communities within Tamale, there is some distrust of Western models. Some believe that psychology is about mind reading and brainwashing. And there's a wider challenge of the stigmatisation of mental illness. In some cases, people with mental health issues have been accused of witchcraft and forced out of their communities.

Traditional methods of care are still practised, says Danaah. These can include inspirational stories of triumph over adversity or the involvement of a spiritual leader to influence thinking. A traditional medicine for mental health, made by boiling the roots of a local tree, can also be offered.

Danaah says Western counselling must be adapted to the local context and fused with traditional methods if it's to make a difference. "The social context means that the Western model of an individual being counselled is often simply not acceptable. For example in some traditional communities women must be counselled with their husband or father present. Women cannot counsel men and people cannot be counselled by someone younger than themselves," he says.

Progress Is Slow

Still, the desire for help is strong. Ori Schwartzman, an Israeli psychiatrist, has established, and volunteers his time, in a mobile psychiatric clinic that visits remote southern Ghana. "In my time, I haven't come across a single [psychologist] in the Ashanti region. People would walk for weeks and arrive at the mobile clinic with their only directions being that the clinic was under the sacred baobab tree."

Though trained in Western psychiatry, Schwartzman believes in working with local cultures. "I was one treatment option out of many, together with magicians, priests. They came to me as they heard that there was a white doctor who could exorcise demons by means of coloured pills," he says.

Back in Tamale, progress to assist the victims of human trafficking is slow. Still, at least there's progress. Ayi has returned home. CIAHT worked with her family, as part of a micro-credit loan program, on a project that involved processing shea-nut butter.

Ayi, now aged 17, finished school and went on to further education, completing a course at a polytechnic and earning a diploma in marketing.

Thai Human Trafficking Victims Reunite with Families in the United States

Teresa Watanabe

Teresa Watanabe is a reporter for the Los Angeles Times. *In the following viewpoint, she considers the vital work of the Thai Community Development Center in Los Angeles that is working to reunite Thai victims of a human trafficking scheme by reuniting them with their families and resettling them in Los Angeles. Watanabe lists the challenges these reunited families will face and the uncertainty over funding for such efforts.*

As you read, consider the following questions:

1. How many plaintiffs are there in the case against Global Horizons, according to the author?
2. How many Thai trafficking victims and their families has the Thai Community Development Center helped?
3. How many more workers could step forward in the case involving Global Horizons, according to the viewpoint?

Recalling the last time he saw his family, he most remembers the tears shed as he left for what he thought would be a chance to earn more than 25 times his Thai income by picking apples in Washington.

Teresa Watanabe, "Thai Human Trafficking Victims Reunite with Families," *Los Angeles Times*, November 19, 2010. Reproduced by permission.

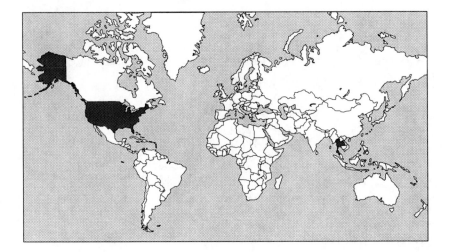

This week [in November 2010], he and his family shed more tears—but this time with joy as they reunited in Los Angeles for the first time in six years after his predawn escape in what authorities call the largest human trafficking case in U.S. history.

"This is the most wonderful moment of my life," the Thai worker said as he hugged his wife and two daughters at the Los Angeles International Airport reunion.

Even as Don and two other workers celebrated their family reunions this week, . . . the daunting challenges of adjusting to U.S. life have only begun.

The Global Horizons Case

The 42-year-old worker, who asked to be known as Don to avoid possible retaliation, is one of about 400 plaintiffs in the federal case against Global Horizons Inc., a Beverly Hills labor contracting firm. Global President Mordechai Orian, an Israeli national, and six associates were indicted in September by a federal grand jury in Honolulu on charges of conspiracy to coerce labor.

Don, for instance, said he was promised monthly earnings of about $2,600. But when he arrived in Washington in July 2004, he said, there was barely any work and he was not paid for at least a month. His passport was confiscated and a guard kept watch over him and about 20 other men, he said.

Orian has pleaded innocent in the case, scheduled for trial in February. He declined an interview request, but a spokeswoman said he "is looking forward to fighting these false allegations."

Even as Don and two other workers celebrated their family reunions this week, however, the daunting challenges of adjusting to U.S. life have only begun, according to Chancee Martorell, executive director of the Thai Community Development Center. The Los Angeles center has worked on the Global case for seven years and has helped resettle more than 2,000 Thai trafficking victims and their families.

The Challenge Ahead for Victims

The families will need to find housing. Don, for instance, rents a single room but will need bigger accommodations affordable on his $8-an-hour restaurant job. His two daughters will need to begin school despite almost no English ability, a task likely to be more formidable for the 16-year-old than for the 6-year-old, Martorell said.

The families will also need to learn to use the public transportation system and get used to myriad other changes, including colder weather, an ethnically diverse society and school cafeteria food.

Beyond the daily needs will be the more difficult psychological and emotional adjustment, Martorell said. Some families arrive here only to find that their husband and father has started a second family. Some men suffer overwhelming stress at the increased financial burdens of providing for a family.

"It's a lot of struggle," Martorell said. "You feel disempowered, frustrated, stressed out."

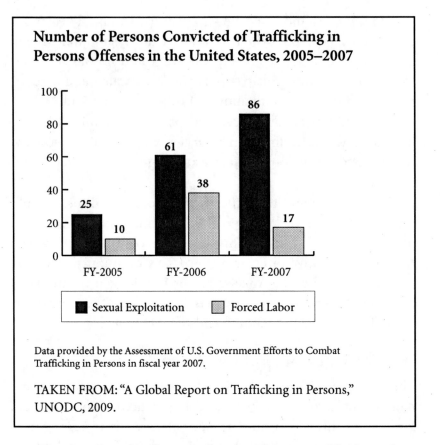

Number of Persons Convicted of Trafficking in Persons Offenses in the United States, 2005–2007

Data provided by the Assessment of U.S. Government Efforts to Combat Trafficking in Persons in fiscal year 2007.

TAKEN FROM: "A Global Report on Trafficking in Persons," UNODC, 2009.

Despite the growing caseload—500 more Thai workers could step forward in the Global case—Martorell expressed concern that the anti-trafficking assistance programs could be shut down if federal funding is not renewed next spring. The U.S. Health and Human Services Department had awarded $17 million to the U.S. Conference of Catholic Bishops to manage cases for foreign victims of human trafficking under a five-year contract that expires in April.

The Thai center receives $100,000 annually under a three-year subcontract with the Catholic conference.

Political Uncertainty Threatens Funding

Martorell said she and other anti-trafficking organizations were concerned that no announcements have yet been made on how to apply for renewed funding and wondered if the process was frozen because of upcoming political changes in Washington [DC], with the House of Representatives coming under Republican control in January.

Kenneth Wolfe, Health and Human Services Department spokesman, said it was not clear how much the new Congress would allocate for the program. But currently, health officials intend to renew the funding, he said.

For now, Don's concerns were more immediate as he reveled in his reunited family.

First, a celebratory feast. Then, settling his daughters into school. The parents, neither of whom finished high school, say their biggest dream is education for their children so they can escape farm labor.

"I never thought this day would be possible," Don's wife said, brushing tears from her eyes. "I had to work hard all of my life, and I want my children to have better opportunities."

Nigerian Female Victims of Sex Traffickers Must Be Educated About Voodoo

Asumpta Lattus

Asumpta Lattus is a journalist. In the following viewpoint, she asserts that Nigerian trafficking networks often use voodoo to intimidate and manipulate their victims into prostitution and other sex work, hampering attempts to combat the crime. Lattus claims that it takes a lot of patience and experience for law enforcement officers to break the hold voodoo oaths have on the victims; quite often these women are offered political asylum because they are targeted by crime syndicates and other criminal elements.

As you read, consider the following questions:

1. How many of the Nigerian prostitutes caught working in Germany were victims of human trafficking, according to the author?
2. How is voodoo used to manipulate Nigerian women, according to the viewpoint?
3. Why does Lattus say many Nigerian trafficking victims return to prostitution after escaping it?

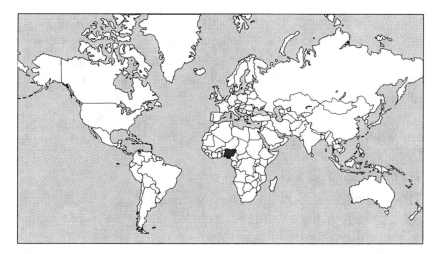

A recent investigation of 600 brothels by the German Federal Criminal Police [Office] uncovered at least 170 Nigerian women working illegally as prostitutes. Authorities determined that 50 of them were victims of human trafficking.

Nigeria is one of many countries to have signed the United Nations protocol against human trafficking. But some Nigerian women as young as 15 are still smuggled to Germany and elsewhere in Europe to work in the sex trade.

Federal Police Inspector Markus Steiner has been checking on the brothels around Frankfurt's central train station, where the city's red-light district is located.

"This is the neighborhood where a girl from a village in Nigeria arrives. In a foreign city where neither the language nor the culture is known to her, where fighting is normal and where even a German person would be uncomfortable," Steiner told Deutsche Welle.

One brothel he visits, a huge, red-lit house topped by sculptures of nude women, has a parking lot full of posh cars.

Steiner said that more than 140 women work there, but the number of prostitutes working each day in the neighborhood around the train station totals about 500.

"At the moment we might not find any African prostitutes, well no Nigerians, anyway," Steiner said. "For us this is a success. But one has to admit that just because no Nigerian victims are found here, that doesn't mean there are fewer victims of human trafficking. It just means that the victims have been sent to other cities like Hanover, Hamburg, Stuttgart, Munich and elsewhere in Germany."

The Voodoo Oath

The Nigerian trafficking networks frequently use a set of traditional beliefs, commonly referred to in the West as voodoo, to intimidate and manipulate their victims.

Belief in voodoo is very strong in parts of Nigeria, and the women are often forced to make an oath by one of the religion's priests, in which they swear obedience to their trafficker or pimp.

Most of the illegal Nigerian prostitutes caught by the police have a lot of stories to tell, but getting them to talk can be difficult. It takes a lot of experience and patience for police to get the real truth from these women—and only then are they able to help them. Because the police are aware of the dangers for trafficking victims who return home, the women are offered political asylum.

> *The Nigerian trafficking networks frequently use a set of traditional beliefs, commonly referred to in the West as voodoo, to intimidate and manipulate their victims.*

Barriers to the Truth

Ritha Ekweza has been through this process. She began working as a prostitute in Germany in September 2007. After being caught, she testified in court in Frankfurt against her sponsor. After the trial, she explains with tears in her eyes how painful it was to have to recall everything she underwent during her time as a prostitute.

"It is not easy to stand and say something, but the thing is, when they bring the girls here, they will just tell them that everything is good, everything is easier, but when you come here it's not the same situation," said Ekweza. "They will bring you and take advantage of you."

Once Ekweza was brought to Europe, her traffickers informed her that she had to pay back some 60,000 euros ($82,000) to them for her flight and other expenses. She worked as a prostitute seven days a week, sometimes attending to more than 18 men a day, to pay off the debt.

In May 2008, she was jailed in Frankfurt for being an illegal prostitute. But together with police and a local women's rights NGO [nongovernmental organization], she overcame her fear of breaking the voodoo oath. She now works as a hairdresser, and has started a family. She still receives counseling from a local NGO called FIM, or Women's Rights Are Human Rights. Ekweza is one of more than 900 African women the organization serves as clients each year.

"We try to stabilize her, socially and psychologically," said Elvira Niesner, a coordinator with FIM. "We look [to make sure] that she feels secure. That is very important, and she will get the money from the officials to survive."

But the biggest challenge remains that of countering the belief in voodoo, which complicates efforts to stop human trafficking from Nigeria. Although police are able to help some women escape from the traffickers, most end up returning to prostitution.

They still want to fulfill their promise of paying back the 60,000 euros that they made in front of a priest in Nigeria.

The United States Needs to Stop Detaining Victims of Human Trafficking

Alison Parker and Meghan Rhoad

Alison Parker is the director of Human Rights Watch's US Program and Meghan Rhoad is a researcher in the Women's Rights Division of the organization. In the following viewpoint, a letter to the US Department of State on the 2010 "Trafficking in Persons Report," the authors describe numerous cases of victims of human trafficking in the United States being held in US Immigration and Customs Enforcement (ICE) detention facilities. Parker and Rhoad argue that measures should be put in place to identify and release these victims, because detention further threatens their mental and physical health and violates the objectives of US anti-trafficking laws.

As you read, consider the following questions:

1. In the case of Lydia, what was she forced to do?
2. According to the authors, how did Loretta end up in the United States?
3. How old was Nina when she was trafficked into Texas, according to the viewpoint?

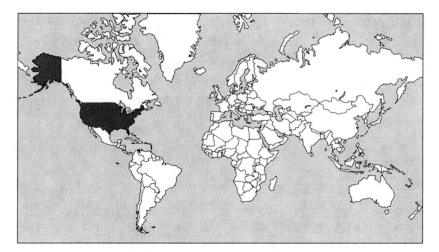

It is our understanding that it is the position of the United States government that victims of trafficking are rarely, if ever, held in US Immigration and Customs Enforcement (ICE) detention facilities. However, in the course of research for numerous reports on immigration enforcement activities, Human Rights Watch has been confronted with cases in which trafficking victims have in fact been detained, sometimes at great length. We provide the following summaries of several cases as examples of the accounts relayed to us by legal service providers throughout the United States.

Ramona

Ramona V., a legal permanent resident, was trafficked by operators of an upscale prostitution ring in the Washington, DC, area. Told by the traffickers that she would be given a job dancing, she was forced to have sex with clients for a period of at least six months. Ramona V. attempted escape from the traffickers by jumping from a moving vehicle. The escape attempt failed and resulted in injuries requiring medical attention. She was arrested twice on prostitution charges and subsequently held in immigration detention for approximately four months in early 2009. While in ICE custody, Ramona was transferred out of the DC area, first up the East Coast and then to Texas. Due to fear that the information would get back to her traffickers, Ramona V. was extremely hesitant to discuss the trafficking, even with her attorney, and spent her time in the detention facilities without talking to mental health counselors.

John

John B. was brought to the US by traffickers in February 2009 under the visa waiver program. He was forced to perform masonry and paving work in various states along the East Coast. His bosses moved him and other workers from his home country between hotels every few weeks. John B. was prohibited from having relationships outside of work and was physically abused when he tried to do so. When he attempted to escape, his traffickers threatened to kill him and his family if he did not return to work. John B. was finally able to successfully escape from his traffickers with the assistance of Good Samaritans. He was then apprehended by immigration authorities and detained in Texas in August 2009. He spent nearly a month in ICE detention, during which he was hospitalized multiple times for cardiac problems. He was released on an order of supervision due to his medical condition, after which he was issued a final removal order.

Lydia

As a young adolescent, Lydia N. left her home in rural Guatemala to escape abuse from her father. After failing to find work in Guatemala City, Lydia N. paid smugglers to take her across the border into the US in May 2007, at which time she was 15 years old. Upon arriving in Houston, the smugglers demanded additional money from her and made her work in a strip club for 15 days. She ran away when they attempted to take her to a party where she was told she would be made to act as a prostitute. Lydia N. traveled to Boston and held a variety of jobs there before being picked up by police on a traffic stop in the summer of 2009. She was taken into immigration custody and held in a juvenile facility for one week before being transferred to an adult contract immigration detention facility on her 18th birthday. At the time the legal service provider met Lydia N. in September 2009, she had been in adult immigration detention for one month. Subsequent developments in her case are not known.

Diana

Diana O. was 17 when she came from Honduras to Mexico. In Mexico, she was held by the Zetas drug cartel before being taken across the border into the US. Found abandoned in a trailer in Texas by Border Patrol, she had been raped repeatedly by people paying money to her traffickers and had been forced to carry drugs. Detained in August 2009, Diana O. had by then turned 18 but told the authorities she was a minor due to her fear of being held in an adult facility. After one month in juvenile detention, verification of her birth certificate revealed that she was 18 and Diana O. was transferred by ICE to an adult detention facility in September 2009. She was held at the adult facility for three to four weeks before being released on bond. In contrast to the juvenile facility operated by the Office of Refugee Resettlement, the adult facility did not provide appropriate mental health services. Her attorney reports that she perceived the adult facility to be particularly traumatizing for Diana O. as compared with other clients who were not trafficking victims. Diana O. began calling her attorney every day and crying on the phone. In February 2010, Diana O. was granted a U visa.

Loretta

Loretta D. traveled from her country to another country in South America to meet someone whom she had connected with through an online dating website. This person sent two men to meet her who kidnapped her and informed her that she would never go back to her home country. She was told she was being "sold" as she passed from group to group of people through several different countries. On reaching the US border, she was raped in the course of crossing into Arizona and called out to the Border Patrol for help. She was detained for a month beginning in March 2009, first in an immigration service processing center and then in a county jail under contract with ICE. After her case came to the attention of attorneys, ICE agreed to investigate the trafficking claim. ICE's main interview with Loretta D. was conducted by a deportation officer. Her attorney requested to be present and reports that the environment was very antagonistic: while the officer was seated, no chairs were provided for the client or the attorney until they insisted on them; the questioning was conducted in an aggressive manner; and the interview was cut off as soon as the officer believed he had found an inconsistency in her story (one which the attorney said could have been reconciled with an otherwise credible claim of trafficking). At the same time, Loretta D. was contending with trauma. Her attorney reports that she greatly feared moving into the county jail where she had been told the traffickers had operatives and would cry hysterically when the attorneys visited. Although her distress abated after moving into the county jail without event, she remained concerned for the safety of her family and decided to agree to deportation after ICE declined to pursue her trafficking claim.

Florence

Florence N. was detained by immigration authorities in July 2006 when she was 16 years old. She had been trafficked from Mexico into the US in 2005 by two men who were brothers and a woman after agreeing to take another woman's place on a trip to the US that was supposed to lead to a job as a waitress. She was held in the US for a year as a domestic worker

US Human Trafficking Victim Assistance Efforts

- Sixteen of ICE's [Immigration and Customs Enforcement's] 26 special agent in charge offices nationwide have hired full-time victim specialists to date—complementing the work of ICE's 350 collateral duty victim assistance coordinators and one full-time child forensic interview specialist.

- ICE has designated 39 human trafficking experts—at least one in every ICE special agent in charge office. These individuals are specially trained to handle human trafficking leads, address urgent victim needs appropriately, and serve as designated points of contact for local officers and leads generated through the Law Enforcement Support Center.

- CBP [US Customs and Border Protection] has produced informational "tear" cards, "shoe" cards, and posters targeting potential victims of human trafficking. These materials connect victims to crisis support and sustained social services for trafficking victims.

US Immigration and Customs Enforcement,
"Fact Sheet: DHS Blue Campaign,"
November 16, 2010.

before someone called the police and they began an investigation into the captors for abduction, domestic violence, and sexual violence. Florence N. was held in ICE custody for a year, first in a shelter and then, after giving birth to the child of one of her captors, in a group home in Arizona specifically for mothers. She was released on her own recognizance in April 2007 and has recently been approved for a T visa.

Nina

Nina S. was trafficked into Texas from El Salvador in 2004 at the age of 15. She had been told by the traffickers that they would provide her transport for $800 which she could pay by working once she reached the US. On arriving, she was made to work in a bar and turn over her wages to the trafficker. She came into ICE custody in 2004 and was put into removal proceedings. However, she was released and caught by her traffickers and moved to Phoenix. In the meantime, an order of removal was issued in absentia. Nina S. was again told to work in a bar and turn over her wages. Nina S. estimated that she turned over approximately $20,000 in wages to her trafficker between her arrival in the US and her second apprehension by ICE. In November 2005, the bar in Phoenix was raided by ICE, resulting in the detention of more than 100 women and girls. From November 2005 to May 2006, Nina S. was detained by ICE in a shelter for minors. She was then moved to foster care until her 18th birthday. She received a T visa and is now in the process of adjusting to permanent status.

Detaining survivors of trafficking undermines the objectives of the Trafficking Victims Protection [Reauthorization] Act and puts the health of survivors at risk.

Janine

Janine F., a legal permanent resident, ran away from an abusive family situation in New York when she was 17. An acquaintance invited her to California and paid for her bus ticket. On arriving in California, she was forced into prostitution. After six months, she was arrested and held in the custody of child protective services for a week before being sent back to New York on a bus. However, not wanting to return home, Janine F. got off the bus when it stopped in Phoenix. She was at the bus station when the same person who had trafficked her to California pulled up in a car. He said, "You should have known better than to try to get away from me." In Phoenix, he again forced her into prostitution. Following two more criminal convictions for prostitution, she was placed in removal proceedings. Now an adult, she was detained by ICE in an adult contract immigration facility in Arizona for over a year beginning in January 2009. A January 2010 letter from her attorney applying for humanitarian parole did not receive a response. In March 2010, at the age of 22, she was awarded cancellation of removal under the Violence Against Women Act and released.

As the "Trafficking in Persons Report" has recognized, measures should be put in place to identify victims of trafficking and ensure that they are not held in detention. Detaining survivors of trafficking undermines the objectives of the Trafficking Victims Protection [Reauthorization] Act and puts the health of survivors at risk. Detention in the US immigration system has been shown to undermine the mental health of asylum seekers, who, like victims of trafficking, have survived trauma. Unfortunately, as the above cases illustrate, trafficking victims in the US continue to be apprehended by ICE or Border Patrol agents for immigration enforcement reasons, and they, like many other immigrants, can spend months or even years in immigration detention facilities.

We appreciate the State Department's efforts to improve the global response to trafficking in persons and, specifically, to raise awareness of the need to ensure that trafficking victims are not subjected to further trauma by being held in detention. We have been encouraged by recent efforts on the part of ICE to contemplate revisions to its intake and custody classifications for immigrant detainees; however, much more needs to be done, as the above cases illustrate. We look forward to seeing these efforts lead to improvements in the treatment of trafficking victims inside the United States.

Periodical and Internet Sources Bibliography

The following articles have been selected to supplement the diverse views presented in this chapter.

Ben Ando	"Human Trafficking Victims Fund to Be Launched by UN," *BBC News*, March 8, 2011. www.bbc.co.uk.
Liliana Barbarosie	"Helping Victims of Sexual Trafficking Find the Courage to Recover," *Radio Free Europe*, September 8, 2008. www.rferl.org.
Ghana News Agency	"Government to Build Shelters for Victims of Human Trafficking," May 4, 2010. www.ghananewsagency.org.
Viv Groskop	"Not for Sale," *New Statesman*, June 2, 2008.
Nicholas D. Kristof	"Helping Trafficking Victims," *New York Times*, December 15, 2006.
Lucy Newman	"Ghana Trafficking Victims Find Care and Comfort in Numbers," *Guardian* (UK), September 22, 2010.
Malika Saada Saar	"U.S. Should Stop Criminalizing Sex Trafficking Victims," *CNN*, February 5, 2011. http://articles.cnn.com.
Times of India	"Website to Help Trafficked Victims Get Quick Justice," March 6, 2011.
Steve Turnham and Amber Lyon	"Judge Finds Hurdles to Helping Young Victims of Sex Trafficking," *CNN*, January 23, 2011. http://articles.cnn.com.
Karen Zraick	"New Law Allows Sex Trafficking Victims to Clear Names," *New York Times*, August 16, 2010.

For Further Discussion

Chapter 1

1. What countries or regions are discussed in the viewpoints of this chapter as being major centers of human trafficking? What characteristics make these areas more attractive for trafficking, and why does it flourish in these places?

2. What kinds of human trafficking are discussed in this chapter? What kinds of human trafficking exist in the United States?

Chapter 2

1. After reading the viewpoints in this chapter, describe some of the political, economic, and social factors that contribute to the practice of human trafficking.

2. How has the global economic crisis contributed to the spread of human trafficking? Use information from the viewpoints in this chapter to inform your answer.

Chapter 3

1. There have been a number of strategies employed to curb the problem of human trafficking. A number of them are discussed in this chapter. Which two seem particularly effective? Which do you feel would work in your community?

2. One of the viewpoints in this chapter makes the point that a culture of sexual objectification leads to the exploitation of women and sex trafficking. Do you agree with this assertion? If so, how can governments, communities, and individuals address this problem?

Chapter 4

1. What challenges do governments, international organizations, nongovernmental organizations, and communities face in helping the victims of human trafficking? Use the viewpoints in this chapter to inform your answer.

Organizations to Contact

The editors have compiled the following list of organizations concerned with the issues debated in this book. The descriptions are derived from materials provided by the organizations. All have publications or information available for interested readers. The list was compiled on the date of publication of the present volume; the information provided here may change. Be aware that many organizations take several weeks or longer to respond to inquiries, so allow as much time as possible.

Amnesty International (AI) USA

5 Penn Plaza, New York, NY 10001

(212) 807-8400 • fax: (212) 627-1451

e-mail: aimember@aiusa.org

website: www.amnesty.org

Amnesty International (AI) USA is one of the country divisions that makes up one of the premier independent human rights organizations in the world. AI, established in 1961, is made up of 2.8 million members, supporters, and activists who work together to address human rights abuses in more than 150 countries and territories. AI members and activists mobilize letter-writing campaigns; mass demonstrations; vigils; and direct lobbying efforts on behalf of individuals and groups being oppressed, tortured, trafficked, and imprisoned for political, economic, social, or cultural reasons. Every year AI publishes the influential *State of the World's Human Rights* report, which assesses the global state of human rights. It also publishes monthly e-newsletters including *Amnesty International Magazine.*

Coalition Against Trafficking in Women (CATW)

PO Box 7427, Jaf Station, New York, NY 10116

fax: (212) 643-9896

e-mail: info@catwinternational.org
website: www.catwinternational.org

The Coalition Against Trafficking in Women (CATW) is a nongovernmental organization that advocates for the human rights of women and promotes policies that fight the sexual exploitation and sex trafficking of women around the world. CATW shines a light not only on forced prostitution and pornography, but also on sex tourism and the practice of mail-order marriages. Much of the organization's work involves education in areas affected by the practice of sex trafficking, focusing on instructing young girls and boys on how to prevent falling victim to predators. It also trains teachers, law enforcement personnel, policy makers, and local officials on how to prevent human trafficking in their communities. In addition, CATW works closely with local and national governments to pass tighter laws against sexual exploitation and sex trafficking. The CATW website offers access to fact sheets, congressional testimony, personal accounts of sex trafficking, articles, and speeches.

Coalition to Abolish Slavery & Trafficking (CAST)
5042 Wilshire Boulevard #586, Los Angeles, CA   90036
(213) 365-1906 • fax: (213) 365-5257
e-mail: info@castla.org
website: www.castla.org

The Coalition to Abolish Slavery & Trafficking (CAST) is a nongovernmental advocacy organization that provides assistance to the victims of human trafficking and forced labor around the world. Its mission is to bring attention to the issue through media outreach and public education, with the ultimate aim of allowing victims to feel empowered. CAST also works to fight forced labor and human trafficking by building coalitions between law enforcement and local communities; one recent example of such cooperation is the Los Angeles Metropolitan Task Force on Human Trafficking, which brings together Los Angeles government officials, law enforcement personnel, and community activists to address the problem in

Los Angeles. CAST publishes a monthly e-newsletter, *Seeds of Renewal*, which explores recent developments in the fight against human trafficking and provides up-to-date news on events and campaigns.

Equality Now
PO Box 20646, Columbus Circle Station
New York, NY   10023
fax: (212) 586-1611
e-mail: info@equalitynow.org
website: www.equalitynow.org

Equality Now is an advocacy organization that works to protect and promote the human rights of women around the world. It documents violence and discrimination against women in a variety of contexts and coordinates with other human rights groups and activists to address it. One of the organization's most important missions is to bring international attention to the issue of sex trafficking. Equality Now is currently working on several campaigns, such as eradicating female genital mutilation (FGM), eliminating sex trafficking, and empowering women politically and economically. On the Equality Now website, readers have access to press releases, press clips, and fact sheets on current campaigns.

Free the Slaves (FTS)
1320 Nineteenth Street NW, Suite 600
Washington, DC   20036
(202) 775-7480 • fax: (202) 775-7485
e-mail: info@freetheslaves.net
website: www.freetheslaves.net

Free the Slaves (FTS) is an international nongovernmental organization working to end slavery worldwide. One of the group's primary responsibilities is compiling accurate research on the problem in order to create viable and effective programs to combat it. Such research functions to educate policy makers and the public on the scope of the problem in the United States and around the world. A few of the recent publications available on the organization's website include *Ending*

Slavery: How We Free Today's Slaves, Hidden Slaves: Forced Labor in the United States, and *Recommendations for Fighting Human Trafficking in the United States and Abroad.* The website also features video, film, the FTS blog, and other resources for teachers, policy makers, activists, and the media.

Human Rights First
222 Seventh Avenue, 13th Floor, New York, NY 10001
(212) 845-5200 • fax: (212) 845-5299
e-mail: feedback@humanrightsfirst.org
website: www.humanrightsfirst.org

Human Rights First is an independent, international human rights organization that advances human rights through accurate research and reporting on human rights abuses worldwide, advocacy for victims, and coordination with other human rights organizations. The group is focused in five key areas: crimes against humanity, fighting discrimination, aiding human rights activists, refugee protection, and advocating for fair legal protections. To that end, Human Rights First offers a series of in-depth studies on such issues, including recent reports on anti-Semitism in Europe, oppressive government counterterrorist measures in Uzbekistan, and China's role in the Sudanese conflict. It also provides an e-newsletter, *Rights Wire*, which examines issues in the human rights field.

Human Rights Watch (HRW)
350 Fifth Avenue, 34th Floor, New York, NY 10118
(212) 290-4700 • fax: (212) 736-1300
e-mail: hrwpress@hrw.org
website: www.hrw.org

Founded in 1978, Human Rights Watch (HRW) is a nonprofit, independent human rights group that researches and publishes more than one hundred reports in order to shed light on pressing human rights abuses. Often working in difficult situations—including those controlled by oppressive and tyrannical governments—HRW strives to provide accurate and impartial reporting on human rights conditions for the media, financial institutions, and international organizations. The group's wide-ranging and thorough reports can be accessed on the HRW website. Interested viewers can also access video, audio, podcasts, photo essays, and photo galleries.

International Labour Organization (ILO)
4 Route des Morillons, Geneve 22   CH-1211
  Switzerland
(+41) 022 799 6111 • fax: (+41) 022 798 8685
e-mail: ilo@ilo.org
website: www.ilo.org

The International Labour Organization (ILO) is the United Nations agency responsible for formulating and overseeing international labor standards. The ILO strengthens social and legal protection for workers and strives to open a productive dialogue on work-related issues. There are a wide range of publications from the ILO available on the organization's website including *World of Work* magazine, a periodical released three times a year that explores labor issues such as forced labor and the rights of undocumented workers. The *ILO Publications Catalogue* provides a full listing of books, working papers, and research studies every year.

International Organization for Migration (IOM)
17 Route des Morillons, Geneve 19   CH-1211
  Switzerland
(+41) 22 717 9111 • fax: (+41) 22 798 6150
e-mail: hq@iom.net
website: www.iom.int

The International Organization for Migration (IOM) is an intergovernmental organization that works with governments and nongovernmental organizations to facilitate humane and orderly migration and protect the rights of migrants all over the world. One of IOM's aims is to advance international cooperation on migration issues. It also provides humanitarian assistance to refugees and migrants. The IOM website offers access to the latest research on migration issues, policy briefs, research papers, articles, fact sheets, speeches, and videos. In addition, there are also links to information on recent books and world migration reports, as well as links to issues of *Migration* magazine, a periodical focusing on migration issues.

International Partnership for Human Rights (IPHR)
Boulevard Bischoffsheim 11, 8th Floor, Brussels 1000
  Belgium
+32 22 76145
e-mail: IPHR@IPHRonline.org
website: www.iphronline.org

The International Partnership for Human Rights (IPHR) is a nonprofit human rights organization made up of practitioners and activists dedicated to promoting human rights around the world. IPHR researches and reports on human rights abuses and governmental compliance with human right obligations; coordinates policy on the issue with international organizations, nongovernmental groups, and local activists; and develops and implements projects that advance the global state of human rights. The IPHR website features access to various reports, studies, letters, press releases, and news articles on relevant topics.

Polaris Project
PO Box 53315, Washington, DC 20009
(202) 745-1001 • fax: (202) 745-1119
e-mail: info@polarisproject.org
website: www.polarisproject.org

Polaris Project is a nonprofit organization working to eradicate all forms of human trafficking and modern-day slavery. The group focuses on several key areas: offering comprehensive services to trafficking victims, such as transitional housing information and health services; training officials to identify and fight trafficking in their communities and companies; public outreach; and strategic lobbying for effective anti-trafficking policies. The group also operates the National Human Trafficking Hotline, which provides assistance to community members, law enforcement personnel, government officials, and field practitioners. The group's blog, *The North Star*, can be found on the Polaris Project website, which also features news updates, video, and media information.

Shared Hope International

PO Box 65337, Vancouver, WA 98665
(866) 437-5433
e-mail: savelives@sharedhope.org
website: www.sharedhope.org

Shared Hope International is a nonprofit organization created in 1998 to eradicate sex trafficking of women and children through education and public outreach. The group has three main missions: create public awareness about the crime in order to better prevent it; rescue women and children from sexual slavery and restore them to a safe and supportive environment; and bring justice to victims by prosecuting the perpetrators. Shared Hope publishes *The National Report on Domestic Minor Sex Trafficking: America's Prostituted*, which offers a comprehensive assessment of the child sex trafficking problem in the United States, and *DEMAND: A Comparative Examination of Sex Tourism and Trafficking in Jamaica, Japan, the Netherlands, and the United States*.

Stop the Traffik

75 Westminster Bridge Road
London, United Kingdom SE1 7HS
(+44) (0)207 921 4258
e-mail: info@stopthetraffik.org
website: www.stopthetraffik.org

Founded in 2006, Stop the Traffik is an international coalition of human rights groups, communities, and activists devoted to eliminating the practice of human trafficking. To accomplish this goal, it educates policy makers and individuals on the crime; advocates for strong and effective laws against the practice and the full implementation of anti-trafficking laws that already exist; and helps victims of trafficking. Stop the

Traffik provides informational and training materials on the organization and its recent campaigns through its website. Films, video, brochures, and a blog can also be accessed on the Stop the Traffik website.

United Nations Office on Drugs and Crime (UNODC)
Vienna International Centre, Wagramer Strasse 5
Vienna   A 1400
   Austria
(+43) (1) 26060 • fax: (+43) (1) 263-3389
e-mail: info@unodc.org
website: www.unodc.org

The United Nations Office on Drugs and Crime (UNODC) is the agency tasked with fighting illicit drugs and international crime, including human trafficking and migrant smuggling. UNODC follows the Convention Against Transnational Organized Crime, an important instrument to fight international crime. One of the convention's protocols is the Protocol to Prevent, Suppress, and Punish Trafficking in Persons, Especially Women in Children, which strengthens the tools countries can use against human traffickers. UNODC publishes a range of literature on the subject of human trafficking, including toolkits for government officials, in-depth reports on the problem, training material for law enforcement personnel, and information for students and community activists.

Vital Voices Global Partnership
1625 Massachusetts Avenue NW, Washington, DC   20036
(202) 861-2625
e-mail: info@vitalvoices.org
website: www.vitalvoices.org

Vital Voices is a nongovernmental organization focused on empowering women around the world through identifying, training, and supporting women in leadership and business roles. The aim of Vital Voices is to help create generations of independent, self-sufficient, and productive women who will enhance their communities and provide opportunities for other women. A key part of its mission is to be at the fore-front of the fight against human trafficking, which is a crime that disproportionately affects impoverished women and young girls. The Vital Voices website offers information on the latest global initiatives to aid women as well as a newsletter and blog that cover news and human trafficking issues. There is also an online store featuring products made by female en-trepreneurs and artists.

Bibliography of Books

Beate Andrees and Patrick Belser, eds.	*Forced Labor: Coercion and Exploitation in the Private Economy.* Boulder, CO: Lynne Rienner Publishers, 2009.
Alexis A. Aronowitz	*Human Trafficking, Human Misery: The Global Trade in Human Beings.* Westport, CT: Praeger, 2009.
David Batstone	*Not for Sale: The Return of the Global Slave Trade—and How We Can Fight It.* New York: HarperOne, 2010.
Carin Benninger-Budel, ed.	*Due Diligence and Its Application to Protect Women from Violence.* Boston, MA: Martinus Nijhoff Publishers, 2008.
Sally Cameron and Edward Newman, eds.	*Trafficking in Humans: Social, Cultural and Political Dimensions.* New York: United Nations University Press, 2008.
Steve Chalke	*Stop the Traffik: People Shouldn't Be Bought & Sold.* Oxford: Lion Publishing, 2009.
Jo Doezema	*Sex Slaves and Discourse Masters: The Construction of Trafficking.* New York: Zed Books, 2010.
Barbara Drinck and Chung-noh Gross, eds.	*Forced Prostitution in Times of War and Peace: Sexual Violence Against Women and Girls.* Bielefeld, Germany: Kleine, 2007.

Obi N.I. Ebbe and Dilip K. Das, eds. *Global Trafficking in Women and Children*. Boca Raton, FL: CRC Press, 2008.

Anne T. Gallagher *The International Law of Human Trafficking*. New York: Cambridge University Press, 2010.

David E. Guinn, ed. *Pornography: Driving the Demand in International Sex Trafficking*. Philadelphia, PA: Xlibris, 2007.

Anna Jonsson, ed. *Human Trafficking and Human Security*. New York: Routledge, 2009.

Siddharth Kara *Sex Trafficking: Inside the Business of Modern Slavery*. New York: Columbia University Press, 2009.

Mike Kaye *Arrested Development: Discrimination and Slavery in the 21st Century*. London: Anti-Slavery International, 2008.

Maggy Lee, ed. *Human Trafficking*. Cullompton, UK: Willan, 2007.

Kimberly A. McCabe and Sabita Manian, eds. *Sex Trafficking: A Global Perspective*. Lanham: MD: Lexington Books, 2010.

Olivia M. McDonald and Renee Sauerland, eds. *Setting the Captives Free: A Compilation of Essays for the Abolition of Modern Slave Trade Worldwide*. Portsmouth, VA: CADIPS Press, 2007.

Shiro Okubo and Louise Shelley, eds.
Human Security, Transnational Crime and Human Trafficking: Asian and Western Perspectives. New York: Routledge, 2011.

Ernesto U. Savona and Sonia Stefanizzi, eds.
Measuring Human Trafficking: Complexities and Pitfalls. New York: Springer, 2007.

Louise Shelley
Human Trafficking: A Global Perspective. New York: Cambridge University Press, 2010.

Leonard Territo and George Kirkham, eds.
International Sex Trafficking of Women & Children: Understanding the Global Epidemic. Flushing, NY: Looseleaf Law Publications, 2010.

Kimberly L. Thachuk, ed.
Transnational Threats: Smuggling and Trafficking in Arms, Drugs, and Human Life. Westport, CT: Praeger Security International, 2007.

Tiantian Zheng, ed.
Sex Trafficking, Human Rights and Social Justice. New York: Routledge, 2010.

Index

Geographic headings and page numbers in **boldface** refer to viewpoints about that country or region.

prosecution of men using prostitution, 132

Identifying trafficking victims

Bosnian efforts, 47

Canadian hotline, 158, 159

Great Britain difficulties, 116

Israeli efforts, 62–63, 64

Japanese efforts, 154

Latin American difficulties, 124

United States efforts, 185

Immigrants, vulnerability to trafficking. *See* Migrants' vulnerability to trafficking

India

trafficking from Nepal, 74–75, 76, 77

trafficking to Kenya, 137

Indonesia, forced vs. chosen prostitution, 67–71

Inquiry into People Trafficking for Sex Work (Australia), 140–141

International Day Against the Sexual Exploitation and Trafficking of Women and Children, 99

International Justice Mission (IJM), 127–128

International Labour Organization (ILO), 77

International Organization for Migration (IOM)

Cambodia work, 145, 147, 148

Kenya work, 137–138

South Africa work, 51

Zimbabwe work, 41, 43

Involuntary domestic servitude. *See* Domestic servitude

Ireland, sex trafficking from Israel, 59

IRIN (news agency), 134–138

Israel, 55–60, 61–64

authorities are not doing enough to reduce trafficking, 61–64

as favorite trafficking destination, 55–60

J

Jakarta Uncovered: Exposing Immorality, Building a New Consciousness (Andriyani), 67–68

Jakarta Undercover (Emka), 68

Janine F. (trafficking victim), 184–185

Japan, 151–155

John B. (trafficking victim), 180

K

Karle, Helene, 129, 131

Kav La'Oved (Israel), 63

Kennedy, Mark, 108–113

Kenya, 134–138

Kimani, Alice, 137, 138

Korea. *See* South Korea

Kumashiro, Yukiko, 41, 43

L

La Strada (anti-trafficking network), 28

Labor trafficking. *See* Domestic servitude; Forced labor

Lagon, Mark, 122–124, 125, 126, 127

LARA (women's organization), 46

Larkin, Thomasina, 151–155

Latin America

coordinated effort needed with NGOs, 118, 119, 127–128

definition of human trafficking, 121